ROLAND HARVEY'S NEW ·BOOK OF· CHRISTMAS

D1450325

The Five Mile Press

THE FIVE MILE PRESS
20 Liddiard Street
Hawthorn Victoria 3122 Australia

First Published 1982
Second edition 1986
© Roland Harvey Studios 1986
Designed by Derrick I Stone Design
Typeset by Meredith Trade Lino
Printed and bound in Japan
by Dai Nippon Printing Company

National Library of Australia Cataloguing-in-Publication data

Harvey, Roland, 1945-
    Roland Harvey's Book of Christmas.

    New. ed.
    Bibliography.
    ISBN 0 86788 080 5.
    ISBN 0 86788 105 4 (pbk.).

    1. Christmas — Juvenile literature. 2. Christmas
    cookery — Juvenile literature. 3. Carols. 4. Creative
    activities and set work — Juvenile literature.
    I. Title. II. Title: Book of Christmas.

394.2'68282

Contents

The Carols

All Carols have been arranged as simply as they allow. The notation is for singing or playing or both. The player has a choice of reading the notes or the chord symbols. Guitarists will probably like the chord symbols best. The piano (or organ) part has been arranged for players with a minimum of instruction. Mostly only two notes at a time are played. Where chords have been written, they will fit small hands. In the main, easy keys have been chosen.

The music doesn't tell you when to play loudly or softly. You should do this yourself, by following the meaning of the words, and in any case, make each verse different. This is what music is all about.

Carols

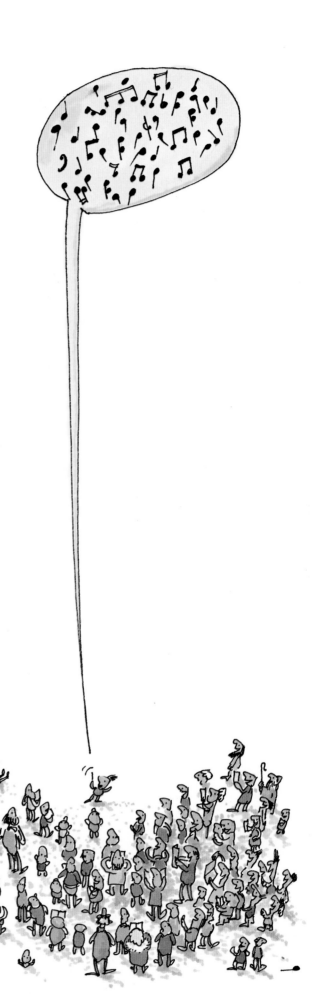

The Spirit of Christmas

Our Christmas festivities go a long way back, many emerging from pagan festivals and ceremonies, celebrating the seasons, the power of the sun and pastoral life. The early Christians centuries ago used many of these old pagan customs to celebrate what they wished to — the birth of Jesus.

Many of our customs and symbols are connected with the Christmas story. The tradition of exchanging gifts, for example, could well have been inspired by the Three Wise Men who gave gold, frankincense and myrrh to Jesus at his birth. The bright star we see in churches, in many religious processions especially in European countries, and of course on the top of Christmas trees reminds us of the star that guided visitors to the stable at Bethlehem. We think of candles as a Christmas symbol, representing the light that Jesus' birth brought to the world. The evergreen Christmas tree tradition started in countries having their dark, cold winter at Christmas time. It reminded people that Christ, like the tree in the midst of winter, brought life and hope for us all.

We all know characters and stories associated with Christmas. Of course the most well-known figure is Father Christmas or Santa Claus, known in different guises and under different names in other countries. Father Christmas demonstrates the spirit of unselfish giving and for us, giving presents is a means of communicating warm feelings to family and friends.

There are many stories to do with the season that deepen our sense of the spirit of Christmas. There is the King Wenceslas figure in the famous carol who saw an old man in need and gave generously. There is the Scrooge character in the story 'A Christmas Carol' by Charles Dickens, who hated Christmas until he was shown what the spirit of Christmas — good will and generosity — really meant, and it made his life a happier one.

Even when times are hard, Christmas is particularly valued as a festival when people come together and enjoy the special feeling which is the Christmas spirit.

This book shows the great variety of ways in which people at different times and in different parts of the world spend Christmas. The more we know of Christmas, in former times and throughout the world, the better we can understand the Christmas Message.

The story of Christmas:

The story of Christmas begins about 2000 years ago......

The Emperor Augustus instructed everyone to return to his home town to be counted for a census.

Joseph and his wife, Mary were visited by an angel of God.

He told them that Mary had been chosen to be the mother of a baby boy to be called Jesus, who would be the son of God, and the saviour of the people.

So Mary and Joseph had to take the long journey to Joseph's home town, Bethlehem, ... travelling on a donkey.

They travelled on......

and on....

and on..

There were some shepherds watching their sheep in the hills near the town. Suddenly there appeared a host of angels, and the shepherds were afraid....

.... but the angels told them not to worry — that there would be a saviour born in the town that night, and that they should go there and worship him!

So they set off.....

....sheep and all...

10

In the east, three wise Kings saw a Star shining more brightly than any other had before .....

...... They set off on their camels, carrying gifts of gold, frankincense and myrrh,

....and rode across hills and deserts, rivers and mountains to see what miracle had taken place!

...and on...

..... until they finally reached the town of Bethlehem.

and rode....

When they arrived at Bethlehem, they found that it was time for Mary to have her baby. But they could find no shelter for her in the town....

and rode...

.... The only place they could find was a stable. It was there that Mary's son, Jesus Christ, was born!

.... until ....

the three Kings arrived at the stable where Jesus was. They fell down and worshipped him, calling him the Son of God; the saviour...

Mary wrapped him in swaddling clothes and laid him in a manger.

...to find the child.

Australia

Christmas in Australia is under the summer skies. The Christmas customs of Australians emerged from the traditions of their ancestors from Europe and elsewhere. Some are kept up with determination despite the often extreme heat and different way of life. They do this partly to preserve their links with the past and partly because they still enjoy them. Father Christmas still wears the hot red, fur-lined suit and boots — but he has an especially red face!

Many people have their long holidays around Christmas and so it is often celebrated at the beach. Some people camp along the shores but never neglect the Christmas dinner; many a miracle is achieved on December 25 on the old camp oven. Australians like having the traditional food, turkey and pudding, although if the temperature soars really high, the food may be cold and a picnic may be had near the water. They may have cold turkey, ham, salads and cold plum pudding with ice cream.

Christmas activities are often outside. It has become a tradition for people to sit out in the warm evenings, in parks and gardens with lighted candles singing traditional Christmas carols — many are still about snow and frosty weather and wintry things, but sometimes particularly Australian songs, about Australian experiences are sung.

Some people have a quiet dinner indoors.....

.... Some have a noisy dinner outside!

Some peop packing

On Chris Carols by Ca is very po

The presents given on Christmas Day should illustrate rather well the 'new' Australian Christmas — beach balls, surf boards, sun hats, beach towels, beach cricket sets inevitably emerge from the pillow case on Christmas morning.

There is much sport to watch around Christmas — tennis and cricket among others, and that interest for people at Christmas has almost become an Australian tradition.

It would not be Christmas for Australians without the decorated tree. Most people have a decorated pine tree, or perhaps a gum. Sometimes enterprising people decorate them with really Australian things — like painted gum-nuts.

After the large dinner, people perhaps have a sleep under the trees or pack the car and go off to the beach to cool off and hopefully not sink from eating too much.

For country people it is a time for relatives to visit from great distances, and perhaps stay overnight. It is also a time for many Australians to think about their families in their former homelands and wonder about what they might be doing.

The roads are packed with cars heading off to holiday resorts

.... because it is summer. Camping is a national Christmas pastime.

Beaches are crowded with people of all ages and nationalities.

13

The Australian Bush

Christmas in the bush has always been a worrying time for the people living far from towns. Little rain, dry bush and sometimes bush fires loom for them at Christmas. Many a Christmas in the bush has been spent beating and thrashing the fires, with the saving rains a present straight from God. In other parts there are great rains that flood the roads and isolate towns for weeks on end. So in early days, the Christmas festive air depended on the rains, sometimes anxiously awaited to break a drought or put out a fire. At other times people might pray for the rain to stop to enable them to visit family in other parts of the country, to buy presents and receive supplies.

Decorations are vases of gum leaves on the tables. Big bundles of green bushes are lashed to verandah posts until the verandah is hidden by a green wall.

Dinner is often on the verandah, usually the coolest part of the house. Sometimes the temperature might reach 44°C but still meat may be eaten hot — roast turkey or perhaps mutton. After dinner everyone may have a snooze, because of the heat and the effects of eating too much!

In early days, when there weren't cars and travel was hard, people would wait for days for the Christmas food to arrive along the rough tracks. People would choose their presents from catalogues, being too far from shops, and wait with excitement for their orders to come. In some cases, lack of supplies necessitated roast young kangaroo, parrot pie, and stewed cockatoos for dinner! In olden times, bushmen, out working far from home would travel by horse for days to be home with their families for Christmas. Relatives would perhaps arrive from Sydney or Melbourne with descriptions of the distant town life.

There is an Australian custom of the bush called 'yarning' after Christmas dinner, with perhaps a pot of tea. Bushmen with so little human contact for months on end, would exchange stories — talk of old times and eccentric pioneers. A bush Christmas was a chance to be with people again, relaxing comfortably on the verandah on a clear, warm night.

Christmas on the Goldfields

Christmas on the goldfields was a time when Christmas was truly a mixture of races and customs from all parts of the world. It was not unusual for the dressed-up Father Christmas to be Chinese, Scottish, Italian or Irish. There were exotic foreign dolls for the children and strange delicious sweets.

Dinner was eaten in the tents and bark huts which were huddled together with holes and clumps of clay all about, or seated outside under the gums with the bush surrounding everything.

Men would try to catch a scrub turkey for dinner. Gold nuggets were sometimes pushed into the plum pudding, often a tinned one, brought at great trouble over many craggy tracks, and cooked, or heated over an open fire. Men, with their wives far away, would try to cook the pudding themselves — boiling it for many hours and, one would think, taking them even longer to digest.

The appearance of a snake or some other visitor from the bush would not have been a surprise at all.

Lots of whisky was consumed if good luck had struck (and even if it hadn't). Quantities of rum were smuggled into the camps and a great deal of riotous activity ensued. The police were very busy at Christmas time on the goldfields.

Christmas would have been usually very hot, with no shady verandahs to keep brows cool. However, in time, ice was sometimes shipped over from Boston to keep food and drinks cold.

It was a particularly good time for the children about the goldfields. The diggers felt very inclined to spend all that gold hopefully dug up, now having wealth they'd never had before. They liked to spend it on presents for children that reminded them of their own at home. For it was a sad time with men thinking of their families far away, and wondering what they were doing at Christmas.

BILLY CAN PUDDING

1½ cups raisins
½ cup sultanas and currants
1 cup sugar
½ teaspoon mixed spice and
    cinnamon
2 cups flour
1 teaspoon bicarb. soda

Combine all ingredients. Mix well
with 500mls of boiling tea. Empty
into greased and floured billy can.
Cover. Stand overnight. Steam 3½
hours.

billycan
pudding

THE DROVER'S PLUM PUDDING

250g rice
sweetened water
sugar
125g raisins or sultanas
handful of nuts

Put rice in saucepan of boiling,
sweetened water and simmer until no
water is left. Add remaining
ingredients. Sweeten to taste.

COLONIAL GOOSE

a leg of lamb
75g fresh breadcrumbs
75g chopped bacon
8 tablespoons finely chopped onion
1 teaspoon finely chopped parsley
1 teaspoon mixed herbs
pinch nutmeg
½ teaspoon lemon rind
salt and pepper to taste
1 beaten egg
milk

Make an incision in fleshy part of leg.
Mix all ingredients well. Stuff the
lamb and tie up with string. Roast
15-20 minutes per half kilo.

colonial goose!

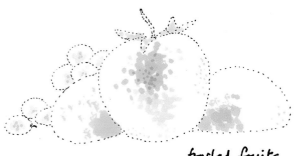

frosted fruits

FROSTED FRUITS
(A good idea for an Australian Christmas dinner)

Use any fruit — oranges, apples,
peaches, plums, grapes or
strawberries. Stir an egg white (or
two, depending on how much fruit
you are using). Brush fruit all over
with egg white. Cover with caster
sugar and allow to dry.
   Pile onto dish.

CHRISTMAS DAMPER

2 cups S.R. flour
½ teaspoon salt
2 teaspoons sugar
1 tablespoon butter
1 cup milk or water (or enough to
   make a medium/soft dough)

Rub the butter into the flour. Knead.
Mould into Christmassy shape — a
wreath or a star. Bake in hot oven (or
in ashes if you are cooking it over a
fire). Cook for 20 minutes until
brown. Serve with butter and jam,
honey or golden syrup.

VEGEMITE PINWHEELS

60g butter
1½ cups S.R. flour
1 teaspoon salt
cayenne
1 teaspoon dry mustard
250g cheddar cheese, shredded
½ cup water
vegemite

Rub in butter with the flour, salt,
cayenne and mustard. Add the
cheese. Mix to a firm dough with the
water. Knead. Roll out. Spread
vegemite over pastry and roll up. Cut
into slices and place on greased
baking tray. Bake at 190°C for 15-20
minutes.

PLUM PUDDING ICECREAM — SPECIAL AUSTRALIAN DISH!
(Very easy)

In a pudding bowl mix together a bucket of icecream (you may have to let it soften a bit first), raisins, sultanas, cherries and plenty of nuts. You can also add a teaspoon of cinnamon if you like spices.

When thoroughly mixed, fasten the pudding lid firmly and place in freezer.

Decorate with *gum leaves* and *gum nuts* when ready to serve.

punch

plum pudding ice-cream

PUNCH

3 peeled oranges
2 sliced bananas
handful of green grapes
handful of stoned cherries
syrup made from ½kg sugar and 6 cups water boiled together for 5 minutes
juice of 3 oranges and 3 lemons
2 cups cold tea
3 cups ginger ale
a large bottle soda water

Thinly slice the 3 peeled oranges and place in a bowl with the sliced bananas, grapes and cherries. Pour over the syrup. Add the orange and lemon juice and let stand in a cool place for 3 minutes. Add the tea, ginger ale, and soda water. Add lots of ice cubes.

Punch

CHRISTMAS SUMMER DRINKS

FROSTY CHOCOLATE
(instead of hot chocolate)

Into each glass put 2 or 3 tablespoons chocolate syrup. Half-fill with milk. Add icecream, then top with milk.

ORANGE AND LEMON FIZZ

1 lemon
1 cup orange cordial
1 bottle lemonade

Extract juice from lemon and grate rind. Add rest of things. Put in iceblocks.

SPIDERS

Put coke or lemonade or any flavour into glasses. Add a blob of icecream.

SUMMER DRINK

yellow cordial
bits of pineapple
ice
1 packet jelly

Make jelly in iceblocks container — lemon or orange jelly are best. Add these when set to the rest of the ingredients.

frosty chocolate

orange and lemon fizz

spider !

sunshine drink

The Three Drovers

This one is very joyful — especially the last line.

A- cross the plains one Christ-mas night, Three drovers riding blythe — and gay, — Looked up and saw a star-ry light, More rad-iant than the Mil-ky Way; And on their hearts such won-der fell, they sang with joy, "No -el, — No-el, — No -el, No-el, No -el, —

2. The black swans flew across the sky,
   The wild dog called across the plain,
   The starry lustre blazed on high,
   Still echoed on the Heavenly strain;
   And still they sang "Noel; Noel!"
   Those drovers three "Noel! Noel!"

3. The air was dry with Summer heat
   and smoke was on the yellow Moon;
   But from the Heavens, faint & sweet,
   Came floating down a wond'rous tune
   And as they heard, they sang full well,
   Those drovers three "Noel! Noel!"

22

Christmas Day

The North-wind is tossing the leaves, —— The red-dust is over the town; —— The spar-rows are un-der the eaves- And the grass — in the paddock is brown; —— As we lift up our voices and sing To the Christ-Child our Heavenly King.

2. The tree-ferns in green gullies sway;
   The cool stream flows silently by:
   The joy-bells are greeting the day,
   And the chimes are a-drift in the sky,
   As we lift up our voices and sing
   To the Christ-Child our Heavenly King.

New Zealand

New Zealand is always the first country in the world to celebrate Christmas as it is the first inside the International Dateline. The 'land of the long white cloud' observes Christmas in much the same way as Australia. The weather is hot and it is the time when businesses close down for the holiday season and most people go on vacation.

During December there are many parties and end-of-year celebrations. School children have concerts and church pageants, pantomimes and carol singing, which are mostly performed out of doors because of the warm weather. The Post Office actually replies to all Father Christmas letters sent by children leading up to 25 December.

Most people hang an Advent wreath on their front door, and inside each home children decorate their own Christmas tree. Each child hangs a stocking at the foot of their bed and holly adorns the rooms of the house.

A sign that Christmas is near is the Pohutukawa trees coming into blossom. They display vivid red blossoms and are known as the New Zealand Christmas Tree.

Families like to be together at Christmas and travel long distances to be with their relatives. At this time of year it is very difficult to get a booking on the ferry which transports people and vehicles from the North Island to the South Island.

The Maori people have made Christmas a very special time. Their celebrations are colourful and happy. They use a special method for cooking their food in the ground. This is called Hangi (pronounced hungi) and is also used by 'Pakehas' (Europeans). A hole is dug and a fire lit to heat up rocks or iron bars. Then the fire is put out and covered with wet hessian. The food is put in the hole on metal trays or chicken wire. The traditional chicken, turkey or duck can be cooked in this fashion along with root vegetables such as kumara (sweet potato). Shellfish can also be cooked in this way.

Many children make their own Christmas cards and decorations. They write to Father Christmas and take great delight in visiting him in large department stores and toy shops. They also make Advent calendars which consist of a cut-out drawing of their own home or school with twenty-five windows. In each window there is placed something common to New Zealand such as a pukeko (a type of hen), a pongo tree (treefern), a kiwi (a flightless bird only found in New Zealand) and pois (a woven ball on the end of a rope used in the Maori dances for elaborate twirling sequences). Or pictures are cut from last year's Christmas cards and stuck behind each window. The window bearing the 25th always has a religious theme (a picture of the Baby Jesus or the Star of Bethlehem). The Maori people and those who have their origins in Europe blend most colourfully and happily, especially at Christmas time.

'Merry Christmas' in Maori is *Merri Krihimete*.

HANGI
(Pronounced *hungi*)
This is a method of cooking in the ground over hot coals. It is also used in a steam hole in the thermal areas of New Zealand. Many Maoris who live in the thermal areas cook like this every day. Pakehas (Europeans) often use this method of cooking when camping or at a special gathering.

You begin by digging a hole and lighting a fire in it. The fire heats up rocks or iron bars that have been placed in the hole. Then put out the fire and cover the rocks with wet hessian.

Wrap the food in foil and place it on metal trays or chicken wire. Lower the trays into the hole.

Use root vegetables, chunks of cabbage, chicken and pork. Cut into sizes that will allow them to cook in the same time. Traditionally, the food was wrapped in green leaves, but now foil is more commonly used.

Cover with more wet hessian and then fill in the hole with dirt and leave to cook.

The Twelve Days of Christmas

On the first day of Christ-mas my true love sent to me A

par-tridge in a pear tree — On the second day of Christmas my

true love sent to me Two tur-tle doves Three French hens Four cal-ling birds and a par-tridge in a pear tree

On the fifth day of Christ-mas my true love sent to me: —

Five gold rings, — Four cal-ling birds, Three French hens,

Two turtle doves, And a par-tridge in a pear tree —

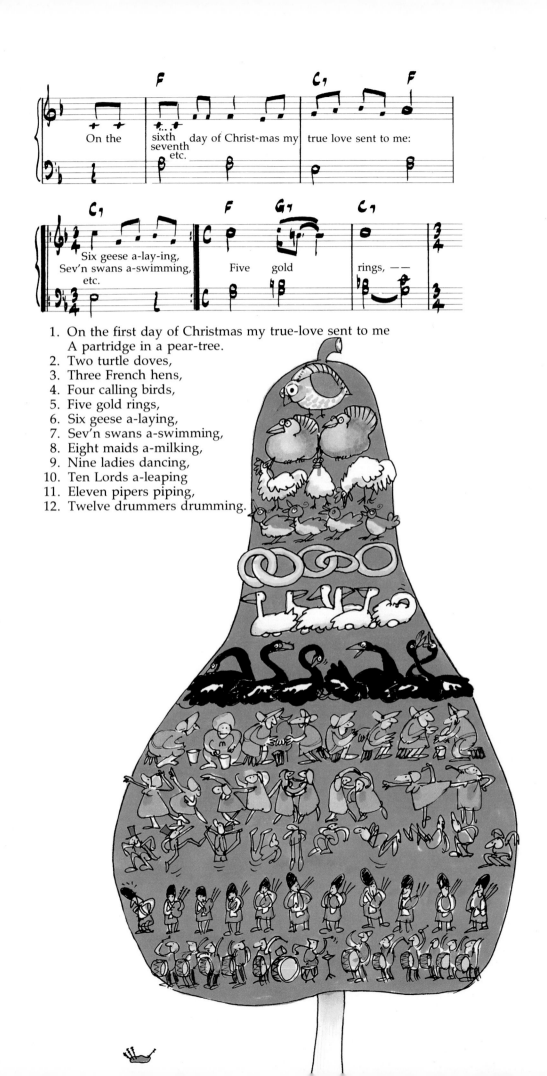

On the sixth / seventh etc. day of Christ-mas my true love sent to me:

Six geese a-lay-ing, / Sev'n swans a-swimming, etc. Five gold rings, ——

1. On the first day of Christmas my true-love sent to me
   A partridge in a pear-tree.
2. Two turtle doves,
3. Three French hens,
4. Four calling birds,
5. Five gold rings,
6. Six geese a-laying,
7. Sev'n swans a-swimming,
8. Eight maids a-milking,
9. Nine ladies dancing,
10. Ten Lords a-leaping
11. Eleven pipers piping,
12. Twelve drummers drumming.

England

Christmas in England began when St. Augustine landed on her shores in A.D. 596, along with 40 monks who wanted to bring Christianity to the Anglo Saxons.

Christmas is a merry and busy time in England. Choirs in church halls practise old carols sung since early days. Groups of singers wander around on Christmas Eve, singing outside doors and windows, in shopping centres and in the underground railway stations where their voices echo through the long tunnels.

Some people act in Mystery or Miracle plays, telling the story of the birth of Christ, first in a lighthearted way and then reverently.

Snow often falls as Christmas shoppers hurry through beautifully decorated streets, which darken so early in this part of the world. And everyone hopes that the snow will fall on Christmas Day—a 'White Christmas' is very special.

Shops and homes are decorated with holly. The green leaves are regarded as a promise that the cold winter will end and the warm sun will return. In early England, holly was hung on the doors of homes where Christ was believed to abide.

People gather in neighbours' homes on Christmas Eve for a warming drink, Christmas wishes and carol singing. Christmas Day is traditionally a family day.

The English were the first people to think of sending Christmas cards. The custom started more than a century ago and it is now popular all over the world.

The churches throughout England are decorated with holly and mistletoe (among other things). An enormous, decorated Christmas tree is put up in the heart of London, in Trafalgar Square, for everyone to admire. It is Norway's annual gift of thanks for Britain's aid in World War 2.

Before Christmas Day, English children sometimes throw their letters to Father Christmas into the fireplace. If the letters fly up the chimney, then their wishes will be granted. They can not be so sure if the letters sit in the grate (but of course they can try again!).

Children hang their stockings by the fireplace so they can be easily filled when Father Christmas struggles down the chimney.

The English have lots of special food at Christmas, often turkey, sometimes goose, chestnuts, apples, mince pies and of course, blazing plum pudding. There is a legend that, one Christmas Eve, an English king found himself lost deep in a forest with hardly any food. Luckily, he met a woodman who offered him his paltry supplies and shelter too. The king's servant, who was hungry too, mixed together what they had between them — suet, flour, eggs, apples, dried plums, ale, sugar, brandy and other oddments. He boiled it in a cloth and they all pronounced it delicious. It is now the essential item on the Christmas menu.

CHRISTMAS PUDDING
(Your mother might need to help with this recipe.)

½ cup plain flour
½ cup fresh breadcrumbs
225g raisins
225g sultanas
120g chopped candied peel
¾ cup brown sugar
120g suet (you can buy this from the butcher)
1 teaspoon grated nutmeg
½ teaspoon salt
2 eggs
4 tablespoons stout
1 teaspoon butter

This recipe is for 1 large pudding or 2 small ones.

Beat eggs. Add stout. Mix all dry ingredients together and mix well. Add eggs and stout to dry ingredients. Melt butter and pour in.

Now everyone must have a stir and make a wish! This is in honour of the 3 Wise Men who followed the star.

Grease basins with butter. Pour mixture into basins. Cover with pudding cloth or foil. Tie with string. Put basins in large saucepan. Fill pan half-way with hot water.

Remember to refill pan about once an hour or more so that the water does not all steam away. Steam for 6 hours.

Let pudding cool. Store away. When you are going to eat, then steam another hour to heat through again.

MINCEMEAT
(You may like to make this mixture — to fill little pies or larger tarts. It keeps a long time and it is not hard to make.)

250g sultanas
250g currants
250g raisins
250g cooking apples
250g brown sugar
250g granulated suet
50g mixed peel
100g ground almonds
½ teaspoon each of grated nutmeg and mixed spice
juice and grated rind of lemon
3 tablespoons brandy, rum or sherry

Peel the apples and remove the cores. Mince or chop finely and mix with lemon rind and juice. Mince or chop the suet and dried fruit and place in bowl. Add the almonds, sugar, and spices and stir well. Add the apple mixture and brandy, rum or sherry. Place mixture in sterilized glass jars (preferably ones with lids). You sterilize your jars with boiling water. Put a metal spoon in each jar before pouring in the water as this will prevent them breaking with the sudden heat.

Plum Pudding

A PECK OF PIKELET

Buy a packet of pikelets. Sandwich 2 together with some squares of chocolate and a few marshmallows. Put in heated oven for a minute or two, until the marshmallows are half melted.

Eat straight away.

Marshmallow Pikelets.

English Trifle.

ENGLISH TRIFLE

1 sponge cake
3 tablespoons strawberry or raspberry jam
1 small glass sherry
1 small glass juice from canned or stewed fruit
1 can fruit (tropical fruit salad, fruit cocktail, raspberries or strawberries)
500mls custard
1 bottle cream (whipped)
125g macaroons
glacé cherries
lots of blanched and split almonds
raspberry or strawberry jelly (optional)

Recipe for custard

2 cups milk
1 teaspoon vanilla
1 tablespoon cornflour mixed with a little cold milk
1 egg and 2 egg yolks
25g caster sugar

Warm milk. Mix eggs and sugar in bowl. Pour milk over egg mixture. Add cornflour. Cook until the custard thickens, stirring constantly (it should become the consistency of heavy cream).

Buy a sponge cake and keep for day or so to get stale before using. Put broken-up sponge into bowl. Coat generously with jam. Cover with half the macaroons. Sprinkle with sherry and fruit juice. Cover with fruit and pour over the cooled custard. Chill for 1 hour. Pile on sweetened whipped cream. Decorate with cherries, rest of macaroons, almonds and cut up jelly.

In the Bleak Mid-Winter

Quite slow and very beautiful!

In the bleak mid-win-ter Fros-ty wind made moan,

Earth stood hard as i — ron, Wa-ter like a stone;

Snow had fallen, snow on snow, Snow on snow,

In the bleak mid-win-ter, Long ——— a-go.

2. Our God, heav'n cannot hold him nor earth sustain;
   Heav'n and earth shall flee away when he comes to reign:
   In the bleak mid-winter a stable place sufficed The
   Lord God Almighty Jesus Christ.

3. Enough for him, whom cherubim worship night and day, A
   breastful of milk, and a mangerful of hay;
   Enough for him, whom angels fall down before, The
   ox and ass and camel which adore.

4. Angels and archangels may have gathered there,
   Cherubim and seraphim thronged the air: But
   only his mother in her maiden bliss
   Worshipped the Beloved with a kiss.

5. What can I give him, poor as I am?
   If I were a shepherd I would bring a lamb;
   If I were a wiseman I would do my part; Yet
   what I can I give him — Give my heart.

34

God Rest You Merry Gentlemen

Not too slow!

2. From God our Heavenly Father
   A blessèd angel came,
   And unto certain shepherds
   Brought tidings of the same,
   How that in Bethlehem was born
   The Son of God by name:

3. The shepherds at those tidings
   Rejoicèd much in mind,
   And left their flocks a-feeding,
   In tempest, storm and wind,
   And went to Bethlehem straightway
   This blessèd babe to find:

4. But when to Bethlehem they came,
   Whereat this infant lay,
   They found him in a manger,
   Where oxen feed on hay;
   His mother Mary kneeling,
   Unto the Lord did pray:

35

I saw Three Ships

2. And what was in those ships all three?
3. Our Saviour Christ and his lady.
4. Pray, whither sailed those ships all three?
5. O, they sailed into Bethlehem.
6. And all the bells on earth shall ring,
7. And all the angels in heaven shall sing,
8. And all the souls on earth shall sing.
9. Then let us all rejoice amain!

The First Nowell

well; No——well; Born is the

King of Is——ra——el.

2. They looked up and saw a star,
   Shining in the east, beyond them far;
   And to the earth it gave great light,
   And so it continued both day and night:
   Nowell, etc.

3. And by the light of that same star,
   Three wise men came from country far;
   To seek for a king was their intent,
   And to follow the star wheresover it went:
   Nowell, etc.

4. This star drew nigh to the north-west;
   O'er Bethlehem it took its rest,
   And there it did both stop and stay
   Right over the place where Jesus lay:
   Nowell, etc.

5. Then did they know assuredly
   Within that house the King did lie:
   One entered in then for to see,
   And found the babe in poverty:
   Nowell, etc.

6. Then entered in those wise men three,
   Fell reverently upon their knee,
   And offered there in his presence
   Both gold and myrrh and frankincense:
   Nowell, etc.

7. Between an ox-stall and an ass
   This child truly there born he was;
   For want of clothing they did him lay
   All in the manger, among the hay:
   Nowell, etc.

8. Then let us all with one accord
   Sing praises to our heavenly Lord,
   That hath made heaven and earth of naught,
   And with his blood mankind hath bought:
   Nowell, etc.

O Come All Ye Faithful

This is a bright Carol too — although lots of people make it sound boring!

Sing, choirs of Angels,
Sing in exultation,
Sing, all ye citizens of heaven above;
Glory to God
In the highest:

Yea, Lord, we greet thee,
Born this happy morning,
Jesu, to thee be glory given;
Word of the Father,
Now in flesh appearing:

Scotland

The Scottish people have their big celebrations on New Year's Day, called Hogmanay. A long time ago Scottish people disapproved of Christmas, believing that too much riotous festivity went on for such a holy day — drinking, eating too much and so on. Nowadays these kinds of things happen at Hogmanay, but they do celebrate Christmas with some interesting customs. There is a superstition that it is bad luck to let the fire go out on Christmas Eve, since that is the time the elves are abroad and only a raging fire will keep them from coming down the chimney.

On Christmas Day, people sometimes make big bonfires and dance around them to the playing of bagpipes. Bannock cakes made of oatmeal are traditionally eaten at Christmas.

SCOTTISH BANNOCKS
(Specially made in Scotland at Christmas)

2 cups oatmeal
1 cup flour
1 teaspoon salt
¾ cup butter or margarine
½ cup boiling water

Mix dry ingredients together in a bowl. Cut in butter with knife until the mixture resembles coarse breadcrumbs. Add the water to the mixture. Mix to a dough. Roll out until quite thin and then cut into rounds (about the size of a jam lid). Cook at 200°C for 10 minutes.

TAFFY-MAKING
(A tradition in Wales and Scotland)

You will need:
1½ cups sugar
1½ teaspoons butter
2 tablespoons vinegar
¼ cup water
1½ teaspoons vanilla essence

The activity of cooking taffy is called a *'taffy-pull'* because you have to pull it! You will probably need a friend to help you 'pull'.

Over a low heat mix sugar, butter, vinegar and water. Stir until mixture dissolves. Cook quickly (be careful) until a bit dropped in cold water forms a hard ball. Add vanilla and pour the sticky mess onto a greased tray.

When the mixture is cool enough to handle, poke your finger in — if the hole remains, roll the mixture into a ball.

Then . . . pull and pull! It will become light coloured and bubbly.

Stretch into a long thin rope, cut into small pieces and store in a box with a tight lid.

Taffy pull

Balulalow

This is another lullaby — so if you wake the baby, it's too fast.

O my — deir heart, young Je — sus sweet, Pre-pare — thy cra — dle in my spreit; And I sall rock thee in — my heart, And ne — ver — more from thee de-part.

2. But I sall praise thee evermore,
   With sang is sweet unto they gloir;
   The knees of my heart sall I bow,
   And sing that richt Balulalow.

43

Wales

The Welsh are great music lovers and every year at Christmas, carol singing is the most enjoyed activity. In the churches, they are sung to the harp. They are sung in people's homes around the Christmas tree and at the doors and windows of the houses.

At Christmas, lots of people gather in the public square for the announcement of who, during the year, has won the prize for submitting the best music for a new carol, and the formal pronouncement of it as the carol of the year. Thus, a new carol is added each year to those already known and sung in Wales.

Taffy making is an essential part of the Welsh Christmas. This involves the making of a special kind of chewy toffee from brown sugar and butter. It is boiled and then pulled so that it becomes lovely and glossy. The Christmas goose is also an institution in Wales.

The Welsh people maintain most of the traditional customs associated with England — holly, mistletoe, pudding, carols, Christmas stockings, oranges, crackers and lots of snow.

In Wales the carolers make their rounds at dawn on Christmas morning, and families wake from sleep and ask them in for refreshments.

Deck the Halls

2. See the blazing Yule before us, Fa la la la la, la la la la.
   Strike the harp and join the chorus, Fa la la la la, la la la la.
   Follow me in merry measure, Fa la la la la, la la la la,
   While I tell of Yule-tide measure, Fa la la la la, la la la la.

3. Fast away old year passes, Fa la la la la, la la la la.
   Hail the new, ye lads and lasses, Fa la la la la, la la la la.
   Sing we joyous all together, Fa la la la la, la la la la,
   Heedless of the wind and weather, Fa la la la la, la la la la.

Ireland

Christmas in Ireland lasts from Christmas Eve to the feast of the Epiphany on January 6, which is called 'Little Christmas'. Their Christmas is more a religious time than a time of fun and revelry.

Lighted candles are placed in windows on Christmas Eve, as a guide and an invitation to all, who, like Joseph and Mary, may be looking for shelter.

The Irish women bake a seed cake for each person in the house. They also make three puddings, one each for Christmas, New Year's Day and Twelfth Night. After the evening meal, bread and milk are left out and the door unlatched as a symbol of hospitality.

St. Stephen's Day, the day after Christmas, is almost as important, with football matches to go to and horse riding meetings. For children, the Wren Boys Procession is their big event. Boys go from door to door with a fake wren (it used to be real) on a stick, singing, with violins, accordions, harmonicas and horns to accompany them. The purpose of the ceremony is to ask for money 'for the starving wren', that is, for their own pockets.

IRISH SHAMROCKS

(To give away — shamrocks are a symbol of good luck in Ireland.)

250g plain flour
250g butter
250g sifted caster sugar
25g ground almonds

Sift flour into basin. Rub in butter. Then add sugar, mixed with almonds. Roll out thinly. Cut into shamrock shapes. Cook at 190°C until golden brown — about 10 minutes. Coat with peppermint icing (to make biscuits green).

Icing

3oz icing sugar
3 tablespoons cold water
1 or 2 drops peppermint essence

Place icing in bowl. Add water and essence and mix thoroughly.

IRISH SODA SCONES

(These rich scones are commonly served during the festive season in Ireland.)

3 cups plain flour
1 teaspoon cream of tartar
1 cup buttermilk
1 teaspoon salt
1 teaspoon baking powder

Stir together dry ingredients and mix lightly with hands. Make a hollow in the centre and add enough buttermilk to make a soft dough. Turn onto floured board and knead quickly and lightly until the dough is free from cracks. Roll out until ½cm thick and cut into rounds. Place on greased oven sheet and bake at 200°C for 15 minutes.

Irish Carol

2. But why should we rejoice? Should we not rather mourn
To see the hope of nations thus in a stable born?
Where are his crown and sceptre, where is his throne sublime,
Where is the train majestic that should the stars outshine?
There no sumptuous palace nor any inn at all
To lodge his heav'nly mother but in a filthy stall?

United States of America

Christmas in America is a very exciting time. Almost all of the Christmas traditions in the entire world can be found somewhere in America because people from many nations have made it their home.

Festivities are on a very grand scale. In the big cities the streets and department stores are beautifully and lavishly decorated. There is lots of shopping, lots of parcels, shining wrappers and ribbons. People spend weeks preparing for the festivities. Carols are practised, there is much cooking and eating, and vast Christmas trees are decorated everywhere — glittering ornaments, popcorn, tinsel, and candy canes are but a few of the often-used decorations. Mistletoe is hung on doorways, homes are decorated with holly and branches of trees, popcorn on string, and bright berries.

In Washington D.C., the capital city, a huge, spectacular tree is lit ceremoniously when the President presses a button and turns on the tree's lights. This tree has become a symbol for the nation. In Boston, the carol singing festivities are famous. The singers are accompanied by hand bells.

Relatives gather together on Christmas Eve and Christmas Day. Presents are often opened on Christmas Eve. The day itself is for church going, and, of course, there is the large Christmas dinner, often had in the middle of the day — usually turkey, though sometimes goose, duck or ham. They have cranberry sauce, nuts and fruit to add to the sense of festivity; then plum pudding or perhaps pumpkin pie, a particularly American pudding.

Church and social groups often celebrate Christmas as a time of sharing and wrap Christmas hampers with lovely food inside, in white paper (because it is so often a white Christmas) and take them around to the poorer people in the community.

There are so many different customs in America concerned with Christmas, some brought by early settlers from Europe and others left over from pioneering days. In the South, fireworks and firearms are let off at Christmas — a custom from early isolated days. It was a way of saying hello to distant relatives and friends.

Ethnic groups keep up their homeland traditions. Hungarian Americans are one group who place even more importance on Church services and caiol singing than other fellow Americans. The many Polish Americans keep up some of their own customs also — for example, the custom of spreading hay on the floor as a reminder of the stable where Jesus was born, is one continued in America.

Large and lavish parades are held in California and in Philadelphia, a procession called a Mummers parade is held, with bands, costumes, dancing girls. This parade goes on for a whole day.

In New Orleans, a huge ox is paraded around the streets decorated with holly and with ribbons tied to its horns.

In Alaska, boys and girls carry around a large star from door to door with them as they sing carols and hopefully are welcomed in for refreshments. Stars are symbols of Christmas in other places in America. In Colorado, for instance, a star is erected which is 150 metres in diameter and can be seen from far and near.

In Arizona, the Mexican ritual called Las Posadas is kept up. This is a ritual procession and play representing the search of Mary and Joseph for room at the inn. Families play the parts and visit each other's houses enacting and re-enacting the drama and, at the same time, having a look at each family's crib which they spend much time preparing.

In Hawaii, Christmas starts with the coming of the Christmas Tree Ship, a ship bringing a great load of Christmas fare. Santa Claus also arrives by boat. In California the great man sweeps in on a surf board.

The poinsettia is known as the Flower of Christmas and this symbol originated in America. The plant is a native of Mexico where it grew unnoticed as a weed. But in 1836 it was brought to America and, on being cultivated, it produced vivid red flowers.

Many legends have developed about the poinsettia. One is of a poor child who was very sad because she could not afford a gift for the Virgin Mary. As she approached the Virgin, she tugged at a weed at her feet in an attempt to have something to give. In her hands, the weed was transformed into a beautiful scarlet flower.

PUMPKIN PIE
(A traditional festive American dish)

2 cups plain flour
1 teaspoon salt
125g butter or margarine
⅓ cup cold water

Put the dry ingredients into bowl. Mix in the butter or margarine with fingers until the mixture resembles large breadcrumbs. Add the water. Make into ball. Chill for 10 minutes. Roll out ½cm thick. Line pie dish with pastry.

Filling
1½ cups cooked pumpkin
½ teaspoon nutmeg
½ teaspoon ground cloves
1 teaspoon cinnamon
1 teaspoon ginger
pinch salt
225g brown sugar
1½ cups milk
2 eggs, beaten
½ cup cream

Peel pumpkin. Remove seeds, stew till soft in a little water. Press through sieve and add spices. Put into bowl. Add eggs, sugar, then milk and cream. Beat hard. Pour into uncooked pastry shell. Bake in moderate oven (190°C) until it is set when you poke it with a knife.

SWEET AND SOUR SNOW ONIONS
(This is a classic Italian dish but it is now served with American turkey dinners at Christmas)

¾kg small white onions
3 tablespoons butter
¾ teaspoon salt
¾ teaspoon freshly ground black pepper
2½ tablespoons sugar
¾ cup red wine vinegar (any vinegar will do)
¾ teaspoon flour
¾ cup beef stock

Peel onions, soak in ice water for 5 minutes and drain. Melt the butter in a large skillet, add the onions and sprinkle with salt, pepper and sugar. Add the vinegar. Cover pan and cook for 5 minutes over high heat. Lower heat and cook for 20 minutes or until onions are tender. Do not stir. Remove the onions to serving dish and keep hot. Add flour to pan juices, blend well, and add the beef stock. Cook for 2 more minutes and pour gravy over cooked onions.

pumpkin pie.

Away in a Manger

As smooth as a lullaby.

A-way in a man-ger, no crib for a bed, The lit-tle Lord Je-sus laid down his sweet head. The stars in the bright sky looked down where he lay, The lit-tle Lord Je-sus a — sleep on the hay.

2. The cattle are lowing, the baby awakes,
   But little Lord Jesus no crying he makes.
   I love thee, Lord Jesus! Look down from the sky,
   And stay by my bedside till morning is nigh.

3. Be near me, Lord Jesus; I ask thee to stay
   Close by me for ever, and love me, I pray.
   Bless all the dear children in thy tender care,
   And fit us for heaven, to live with thee there.

Rise up Shepherd an' Foller

fol — ler,   Rise up, shepherd and fol-ler, —

Fol-ler the star of   Beth — le — hem, ———

Rise up,   shepherd   and   fol — ler. ———

2. If you take good heed to the angel's words,
   Rise up, shepherd, an' foller,
   You'll forget your flocks, you'll forget your herds;
   Rise up, shepherd, an' foller.
   Leave your sheep and leave your lambs,
   Rise up, shepherd and foller;
   Leave your ewes and leave your rams,
   Rise up, shepherd and foller.
   Foller, foller, Rise up, shepherd and foller,
   Foller the star of Bethlehem,
   Rise up, shepherd and foller.

Joy to the World

2. Joy to the world! the Savior reigns;
   Let men their songs employ;
   While fields and floods, rocks, hills and plains,
   Repeat the sounding joy,
   Repeat the sounding joy,
   Repeat, repeat the sounding joy.

3. No more let sin and sorrow grow,
   Nor thorns infest the ground;
   He comes to make His blessings flow
   Far as the curse is found,
   Far as the curse is found,
   Far as, far as the curse is found.

4. He rules the world with truth and grace,
   And makes the nations prove
   The glories of His righteousness,
   And wonders of His love,
   And wonders of His love,
   And wonders, and wonders of His love.

5. Now to the Lord sing praises,
   All you within this place,
   And with true love and brotherhood
   Each other now embrace;
   This holy tide of Christmas
   All others doth deface:

Canada

In Canada, Santa Claus wears snowshoes and has at times been seen in Montreal in a sled pulled by reindeer with Indians on their backs.

Traditionally, Santa Claus arrives on 25 November and visits department stores, shops, schools and parks in anticipation for Christmas a month later. At about this time, pre-baking also takes place, with prominence given to items made from maple syrup, such as sweets, biscuits and gingerbread men.

In Quebec City, in a street known as Carnival Street, the residents all participate in ice and snow sculpturing over the festive season as well as dancing and singing. The sculptures are life-size and usually with a Christmas theme, but they include houses and animals along with castles and famous people.

It is a very colourful time of year: city squares and main rivers are decorated with coloured lights and homes are decked with holly and fir branches. Christmas stockings are placed at the foot of each child's bed and on Christmas morning they are found full of presents.

In Labrador, little children enjoy receiving lighted candles standing in a turnip that has been especially saved from harvest time. In days gone by, the candles were made from reindeer tallow, making them edible along with the turnip.

In Nova Scotia, the highlanders or farmers read psalms in small churches or their own cottages. They sing carols which their ancestors brought with them from Brittany and Normandy two centuries ago. Christmas dishes are flavoured with maple syrup which the Indians taught the early settlers to use.

In the far north of Canada, the Eskimos celebrate the season with a huge mid-winter festival called Sincktuck, meaning 'big dance and present giving party'. They dance in their elaborate fur-trimmed costumes, adorn themselves with ivy and feast on rare delicacies. The highlight of the party is the giving and receiving of presents. For the Eskimo this is a time of goodwill and merriment for all.

In British Columbia, the Christmas dinner is highlighted by the inclusion of fabulous seafood such as oysters, shellfish, King Crab, shrimps and pink salmon. In addition to the wealth of seafood, there are berries, such as gooseberries, blackcurrants, loganberries and blackberries. These fruits are prepared in the summertime and used extensively in winter/Christmas cooking.

Traditionally, the Canadian Christmas dinner may include the following:

Fresh oyster soup
Tourtiere

Roast turkey with stuffing and gravy
Mashed potatoes
Mashed carrots and turnips
Green vegetables such as peas
Cranberry sauce

Buche de Noël

Cheese and fruit

The festivities conclude on New Year's Eve with most people building huge bonfires with logs. They sing and dance to music into the early hours of the new year, and often drink champagne and eat fondue.

MEAT PIE
(Tourtière)

2 kg lean, ground pork
1 medium onion, chopped
salt and pepper
¼ teaspoon ground cloves
1 bay leaf
¼ cup boiling water
short pastry for 2 crusts

Put first six ingredients in a saucepan and mix well. Add boiling water and simmer uncovered for 20 minutes, stirring occasionally. Remove the bay leaf and skim off any fat.

Roll out half the pastry and line a 22 cm pie plate. Place the filling in the pie plate and cover with the remaining pastry. Make an incision in the centre to allow steam to escape.

Bake in a preheated 180°C oven for 30 minutes, or until the crust is golden. Serve hot.

(Serves 4-5)

MAPLE SUGAR PIE
(Tarte au sucre d'érable)

2 cups chopped maple sugar
1 cup cream
½ cup chopped nuts

Preheat the oven to 180°C.

Put the maple sugar and cream in a saucepan and boil over low heat, stirring occasionally, for 15 or 20 minutes. Remove from heat and add the chopped nuts. Allow the mixture to cool, then pour into a 22 cm pie crust.

Bake for 40 to 45 minutes.

Pie crust

1½ cups plain flour
½ teaspoon salt
½ teaspoon baking powder
¼ cup butter or margarine
¼ cup vegetable shortening
2 tablespoons sugar
1 egg

Sift the flour, salt and baking powder. Cut in the shortening, broken up into small pieces. Add the sugar and the egg and mix carefully. (If a little extra liquid is necessary, use cream.) Roll out on a surface lightly dusted with flour and press into a 22 cm pie plate.

CIPÂTE
(Six-pâtés)

4 kg pork
4 kg beef (shoulder cut)
2 rabbits
3 chicken legs
4 chicken breasts
2 teaspoons salt
½ teaspoon pepper
2 large onions, chopped
4 or 5 slices of bacon

Bone the chicken and rabbits, saving the bones; cut the meat into cubes. Mix the meat with the onions, salt and pepper. Cover and chill for 12 hours.

To prepare the pie, fry slices of bacon in an oven-proof casserole, then remove them. Put a layer of meat in the hot fat, pour in half the stock and cover with a layer of pastry squares, leaving a little space between each square. Add a second layer of meat and pour in the rest of the stock. Cover completely with a layer of pastry, into which a couple of incisions should be cut to allow steam to escape during cooking.

Bake in an oven preheated to 220°C for ¾ of an hour, then reduce the temperature to 180°C and bake for another 5 hours.

(Serves 14)

Stock

Place chicken and rabbit bones in a saucepan. Add 1 chopped onion, salt and pepper, and enough cold water to cover. Simmer over moderate heat for 2 hours. Strain stock and refrigerate until needed.

Pastry

3 cups plain flour
2-3 tablespoons lard
3 teaspoons baking powder
½ teaspoon salt
½ cup milk

Mix all ingredients thoroughly and divide the pastry into two parts. On a surface dusted lightly with flour, roll out the first half to a thickness of 1 cm. Cut into 2 cm squares. Roll out the rest of the pastry and use to cover pie.

We Three Kings

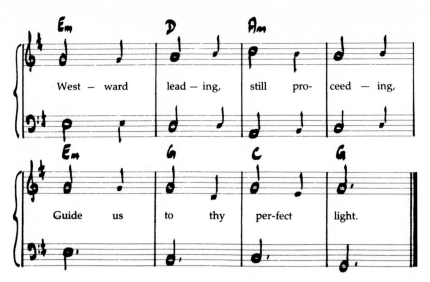

West — ward lead — ing, still pro-ceed — ing,

Guide us to thy per-fect light.

2. Born a king on Bethlehem plain,
   Gold I bring, to crown him again
   King for ever, ceasing never,
   Over us all to reign:
      Refrain

3. Frankincense to offer have I;
   Incense owns a deity nigh:
   Prayer and praising, all men raising,
   Worship him, God most high:
      Refrain

4. Myrrh is mine; its bitter perfume
   Breathes a life of gathering gloom;
   Sorrowing, sighing, bleeding, dying,
   Sealed in the stone-cold tomb:
      Refrain.

5. Glorious now, behold him arise,
   King, and God, and sacrifice!
   Heav'n sings alleluya,
   Alleluya the earth replies:
      Refrain.

While Shepherds Watched Their Flocks by Night

While shep-herds watched their flocks by night, All

sea-ted on the ground, The an-gel of the

Lord came down and glo-ry shone a-round.

2. 'Fear Not,' said he (for mighty dread
   Had seized their troubled mind);
   'Glad tidings of great joy I bring
   To you and all mankind.'

3. 'To you in David's town this day
   Is born of David's line
   A Saviour, who is Christ the Lord;
   And this shall be the sign:'

4. 'The heavenly Babe you there shall find
   To human view displayed,
   All meanly wrapped in swathing bands,
   And in a manger laid.'

5. Thus spake the seraph; and forthwith
   Appeared a shining throng
   Of angels praising God, who thus
   Addressed their joyful song:

6. 'All glory be to God on high,
   And to the earth be peace;
   Good-will henceforth from heaven to men
   Begin and never cease.'

France

Christmas in France is a very religious time and a family holiday. French children receive presents on Christmas Day but adults wait until New Year's Day to give each other gifts.

In the Southern part of France a log is burned in fireplaces in people's homes from Christmas Eve to New Years Day. In times long ago, part of the log was used to make the wedge for the plough as good luck for the coming harvest.

The nativity crib is important for the French. (It was St. Francis of Assisi, an Italian saint — who first thought of the crib and made one). In some regions, French people spend a lot of time modelling figures of the Christmas story out of clay or wood. They also make models of various people in the town like the priest, the policeman, the butcher and many others and put them in the manger too.

On Christmas Eve, the bigger children go with their parents to Midnight Mass where the churches are lit up, hymns are sung and bells resound. The family then has a meal called *le réveillon* which means the awakening (though they must feel rather unawake at that hour) of roast chicken, ham, salads, cake, fruit and wine.

In some parts of France goose is eaten, in other parts buckwheat cakes and sour cream. In Paris, people enjoy oysters, and they have a special cake called *Bûche de Noël,* which is shaped like a log. The Yule log is a special symbol in many countries, representing fire, warmth and light, a symbol of good luck for the coming year.

French children often put out their shoes by the fireside to be filled with presents by Père Noël.
In some parts of France it is St. Nicholas who visits, in others, the Christmas Angel.

PUDDING DE NOËL A LA FRANCAISE
(Christmas pudding as the French have it)

½kg marrons glacés pieces (chestnuts) crushed finely. (You can also buy tins of chestnut puree from supermarkets that will do just as well)
7 tablespoons butter
2 tablespoons heavy cream
8 egg yolks
6 egg whites, beaten very stiffly
vanilla

Crush marrons glacés finely, flavour with vanilla and mix in butter. Dilute with cream. Pour into sieve (you do not have to do this if you are using tinned chestnut puree). Add the egg yolks. Fold in the whites, beaten very stiffly. Pour into charlotte mould and bake at 325°C for 30 minutes. Turn out and when cold cover with the chocolate cream sauce.

Pudding de Noël à la Française

SAUCE CRÈME AU CHOCOLAT
(Chocolate cream sauce)

125g cocoa
½ cup water
1 cup cream
2 tablespoons butter
⅔ cup sugar

Place the cocoa and water in saucepan. Cook slowly until mixed and smooth. Add sugar and stir until dissolved. Just before serving, add, off the heat, the cream and butter. Whip for 2 minutes.

CHRISTMAS LOG (BÛCHE DE NOËL — A SPECIAL TRADITION IN FRANCE)
(This is a simple version of the special French Christmas cake.)

1 packet of chocolate biscuits (chocolate ripple are good)
1 cup of cream
cooking chocolate or cocoa/sugar to colour the cream

Whip cream and melted chocolate or cocoa/sugar until cream is thick and the colour of milk chocolate. Spread the cream between all but 3 of the biscuits and with the remaining cream, cover the log. Cut the 3 biscuits left into fingers to make a twig shape and join to the end of the log. Rough up surface to resemble bark. (Grated chocolate sprinkled along the top would look good.) Decorate with holly.

Bûche de Noël.

Epiphany Cake

FLAN De L'EPIPHANIE
(Epiphany Tart)

For the base:
1 packet frozen sweet puff pastry

For the cream filling:
2 cups milk
60g sugar
2 egg yolks
25g flour
2 tablespoons rum

Choux mixture:
2 cups water
125g butter
4 eggs
pinch of salt

1 packet marzipan

Thaw the puff pastry. Roll out pastry to cover the bottom of a buttered pie dish. Prick the bottom. Roll out marzipan and cover pastry with it.

Cream Filling
In a saucepan, work the flour, egg yolks, sugar. Add the milk. Heat until boiling. Flavour with rum.

Choux Pastry
Boil the water, salt and butter. Pour in the flour in one go, and thicken, stirring constantly, until the mixture comes away at the sides. Off the heat, put in the whole eggs one by one. Mix the cream filling with the choux mixture. Pour into pie dish and put in the "feve" (this means bean in French. Whoever gets it, becomes King or Queen of the day). Cook in a hot oven, 230°C, for about 25 minutes. This galette should be served warm sprinkled with rum.

BUCKWHEAT CAKES
(Special at Christmas in some parts of France — perhaps cook them for breakfast on Christmas morning.)

½ cup milk
2 tablespoons melted butter
1 egg
½ cup plain flour
½ cup buckwheat flour (wholemeal flour will do)
2 teaspoons baking powder
2 tablespoons sugar
½ teaspoon salt

Sift flour, sugar, baking powder, salt into bowl. Add milk, butter and egg. Mix well. Add more milk if necessary, to make the batter as thick as heavy cream. Cook in greased frying pan, using about ¼ cup of mixture at a time.

Angels from the Realms of Glory

2. Sages, leave your contemplations;
   Brighter visions beam afar;
   Seek the great Desire of Nations;
   Ye have seen his natal star:
      Gloria in excelsis, etc.

3. Saints before the altar bending,
   Watching long in hope and fear,
   Suddenly the Lord, descending,
   In his temple shall appear:
      Gloria in excelsis, etc.

4. Though an infant now we view him,
   He shall fill his Father's throne,
   Gather all the nations to him;
   Every knee shall then bow down:
      Gloria in excelsis, etc.

Ding Dong! Merrily on High

very light and bright, with smooth 'Glorias'.

Can you get through 'Gloria' in one breath?

2. E'en so here below, below, let steeple bells
   be swungen,
   And i-o, i-o, i-o, by priest and people sungen.

3. Pray you dutifully prime your matin chime,
   ye ringers:
   May you beautifully rime your evetime song,
   ye singers.

Germany

Christmas in Germany starts with Advent (four Sundays before Christmas). A wreath of holly with four red candles fixed to it is hung in many German homes, and one candle is lit each Sunday before Christmas, the final one on Christmas Eve.

Carols are sung by choir boys called 'the Starlings', often from the Church tower, the sound filtering down through the village streets.

In towns all over Germany, Christmas trees can be seen glittering and glowing. Some German families have several Christmas trees in their homes, one for each member of the family. It was Germany that first started the tradition of decorating trees at Christmas, then other countries did the same. They decorate the tree with lights and sweets — their favourite sweet is marzipan, an almond sweet. They are shaped for Christmas like meat, fruits or toys. Everyone gathers on Christmas Eve for a special ceremony to light the tree.

Many German families make their own gifts. Women and girls do a lot of embroidering — handkerchiefs and cushions particularly. Boys often carve figures from wood and give them away.

On Christmas Eve, the Christkind, a veiled angel with gold wings and a white gown, is said to visit on behalf of the Infant Jesus. She enters by the window and rings a silver bell. A table is set with a plate for each child and it is believed that it is the Christkind who fills these plates with sweets and fruit by morning.

There is a custom in Germany called Knocking Night where people in hideous and fearful masks and costumes go from house to house rattling tin cans, ringing cow bells, cracking whips, throwing small stones against windows and generally being very noisy. Occasionally, a pitchfork is thrust through the open door for food to be skewered onto it. The custom had a little to do with the story of Joseph and Mary knocking on doors of inns, but now it is just something fun to do.

There is an interesting custom in Northern Germany (as well as Sweden and Denmark) called *Julklapp*, meaning 'Christmas Box'. People go about different houses at night, ring the bell, throw in a parcel when the door is opened (let's hope it's not breakable) and dash away before being recognised. The present is disguised in lots of paper or sometimes just a clue is left as to the whereabouts of the present. The longer it takes to work out the giver, or where the gift has been hidden, the better has been the *Julklapp*.

CHRISTMAS STOLLEN
(A German Christmas tradition)

Make dough:
Put in bowl
1 cup warm milk
1 package dry yeast
Let stand five minutes.
Add:
¼ cup sugar
1 teaspoon salt
¼ cup soft butter
2 eggs
Beat thoroughly.
Beat in:
1½ cups plain flour
Let rise for 40 minutes.
Mix in:
1 cup flour

Chill ½ hour. Roll out flat. Cover with ½ cup slithered almonds, ½ cup candied peel, 1 tablespoon grated lemon rind. Knead in fruit and nuts. Shape into oblong. Brush with melted butter and fold double lengthwise. Press edges together. Place on greased oven tray. Let rise to double the size. Bake at 190°C for 35 minutes. Ice with plain icing.

Icing

¼ cup boiling water

Add icing sugar until thick enough to spread. Flavour with vanilla. Ice when stollen is cool. Decorate with slivered almonds and candied peel.

CHRISTMAS STUFFING
In Germany, the Christmas bird is usually duck or goose. It is perhaps the exotic stuffing that makes the roast a really festive one. You could use this stuffing for any bird.

150g goose liver (or any liver)
150g sausage meat
90g breadcrumbs
1 tablespoon chopped parsley
pinch sage and mint
2 eggs
salt and pepper
60g walnuts
90g raisins and sultanas
120g diced apples and pears
30g flour

Blend minced liver and sausage meat with crumbs, flour and beaten egg, then add nuts and fruits with seasoning. Stuff the bird.

Stollen

Silent Night

2. Silent night! Holy night!
   Shepherds quake at the sight!
   Glories stream from heaven afar,
   Heav'nly hosts sing, "Alleluia!"
   Christ, the Savior, is born!
   Christ, the Savior, is born!

3. Silent night! Holy night!
   Song of God, love's pure light!
   Radiant beams from Thy holy face
   With the dawn of redeeming grace,
   Jesus, Lord, at Thy birth!
   Jesus, Lord, at Thy birth!

O Little One Sweet

Good Christian Men Rejoice

Good Christian men, re-joice With heart and soul and voice! —

Give ye heed to what we say: News! News! Je-sus Christ is

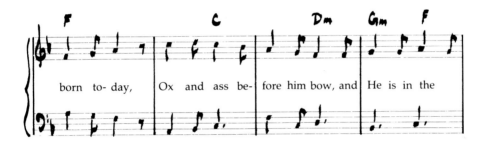

born to-day, Ox and ass be-fore him bow, and He is in the

man-ger now: Christ is born to-day, — Christ is born to-day. —

2. Good Christian men, rejoice
With heart and soul and voice!
Now ye hear of endless bliss:
Joy! Joy!
Jesus Christ was born for this.
He hath oped the heavenly door,
And man is blest for evermore.
Christ was born for this,
Christ was born for this.

3. Good Christian men, rejoice
With heart and soul and voice!
Now ye need not fear the grave:
Peace! Peace!
Jesus Christ was born to save;
Calls you one, and calls you all,
To gain his everlasting hall.
Christ was born to save,
Christ was born to save.

Italy

The Christmas season in Italy goes for three weeks, starting 8 days before Christmas (called the beginning of the Novena). During this time, children go from house to house reciting Christmas poems and singing.

In some parts of the country, shepherds bring musical instruments into the villages, play and sing Christmas songs.

Italians fast for 24 hours before Christmas. They end this after Midnight Mass with a special supper of *Panetoni* (spiced bread) and chocolate.

The setting up of the *presepio* — the Christmas manger — is a very special custom in Italy. There are huge ones in the Churches and many families put up their own at home.

On the feast day of the Epiphany (January 6th) — when Jesus was shown to the world, children normally receive their gifts. According to tradition, the presents are delivered by a kind but ugly witch called Befana, on a broomstick. It seems that when she was told of the birth of Jesus by the 3 Kings, she was busy and delayed visiting the Baby.

She missed the Star, lost her way and has been flying around ever since, leaving presents at every house with children in case he is there. She slides down chimneys, and fills stockings and shoes with good things for good children and, it is said, leaves coal (which is really just a sweet looking like coal) for children who are not so good.

TORTELLINI
(This is the traditional dish served during Christmas, particularly in Northern Italy. To make the recipe easier and quicker, I suggest that you buy the frozen pasta found at most supermarkets.)

1 packet frozen tortellini
125g butter
¼ cup heavy cream
1 cup grated parmesan cheese
freshly ground pepper
1 tablespoon salt

Boil the tortellini in a large pan of boiling salted water for approximately 10 minutes until tender, stirring occasionally. Drain. Place cream, ¾ of the cheese and butter into pan and bring to boil. Pour sauce over tortellini. Sprinkle with parsley and rest of cheese.

AMARETTI
(Traditionally served at Christmas)

2 egg whites
¼ teaspoon salt
1 cup sugar
1 cup chopped blanched almonds
¾ teaspoon almond extract

Add salt to egg whites and beat until frothy. Add sugar gradually, beating until mixture is stiff but not dry. Add almonds and almond extract and fold in gently. Drop almond mixture on buttered and floured baking sheet by the teaspoon, shape into small mounds, leaving room between each mound. Let stand 2 hours. Bake at 190°C for 12 minutes or until they are delicately brown in colour.

TORTE VIGILIA DI NATALE
(Christmas Eve Cake)

1 cup water
1 cup sultanas
¼ cup chopped walnuts
¼ cup chopped almonds
1 cup sugar
½ cup butter/margarine
1 egg
2 teaspoons vanilla
1 teaspoon baking powder
½ cup sifted flour

Mix together water, sultanas, walnuts and almonds in a saucepan and bring to boil. Reduce heat and simmer for 5 minutes. Cool.

Cream butter and sugar. Add egg. Beat well. Add vanilla. Add sifted flour and baking powder to creamed mixture. Add fruit mixture. Blend thoroughly. Pour into well buttered 20cm square tin. Bake at 180°C for 30 minutes.

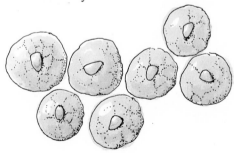

amaretti

torte vigilia

Tu Scendi Dalle Stelle

From star-ry skies thou com-est, — The King of Heav'n fore-told, — Ap-pear-ing in a man-ger, Near fro-zen from the cold, — Ap-pear-ing in a man-ger, Near fro-zen from the cold. Je-sus dear-est lit-tle Ba-by, How I long to make Thee

warm, — To shel-ter Thee from harm! — My heart is filled with

pi — ty for Thy ti — ny form, — My heart is filled with

pi — ty for Thy ti — ny form. —

In Notte Placida

l'an-i-mo a-pri tea sper-   an-za e a d a-mor!   Can-ta-te, po-po-li,

glori a a l l'al-tis-si-mo,   l'an-i-mo a-pri tea sper   -an za e a d a-mor!

da Capo

Greece

In Greece, the people begin Christmas with a 40 day fast, known as Short-Lent. This ends finally, and thankfully, on Christmas Eve. Mass on Christmas Day starts very early at 4 a.m., and ends just before daybreak. After that they have a family meal. Christmas dinner is quite spectacular. The large delicious feast includes suckling pig, roast leg of lamb or turkey roasted on a spit, stuffed with a delicious and very rich mixture of chestnuts, pinenuts, walnuts, rice, meat, onions, tomatoes, raisins and much more. They also eat a cake covered with nuts called 'bread of Christ' with a cross on top made of walnuts, and many other cakes as well — some shaped into animals.

On Christmas Eve, carols are usually sung by small boys to the beating of drums and the tinkling of triangles. They go from house to house and are given dried figs, almonds, walnuts and lots of sweets or sometimes small gifts. They also sing on the buses and travel free for the pleasure they give to the other travellers.

There is a tradition to leave food out — cakes and biscuits — for the *kallikantzeri*, the mischievous goblins who appear from the earth during the 12 days of Christmas.

At Christmas they give very few presents to each other. Instead they give pleasure to hospitals and orphanages with small gifts. Presents are exchanged at New Year and St. Basil is the legendary figure who gives gifts to children.

Another custom is for a priest to go from house to house, sprinkling holy water around to get rid of the bad spirits who may be hiding in people's houses.

Greeks traditionally bake a special Christmas bread. They twist the dough into shapes of farm animals and nail them to the walls of their homes, and there the bread stays for a whole year.

Christopsomo

CHRISTOPSOMO
(Bread of Christ)

2 packages active dry yeast
½ cup warm water
½ cup milk
¾ cup butter
¾ cup sugar
4 eggs
2 teaspoons salt
5 cups plain flour
walnuts
2 teaspoons crushed anise seed

Sprinkle yeast into warm water and stir. Stand until dissolved. Heat milk and butter together until butter melts. Pour yeast mixture, milk and butter into a mixing bowl, add sugar and let cool. Add eggs and beat until smooth. Mix in anise seed, salt, and 2 cups flour. Beat for 5 minutes. Gradually add remaining flour. Turn out dough. Knead until smooth and no longer sticky (about 10 minutes). If necessary, knead in additional flour. Place dough in bowl, butter the top, cover and let rise in a warm place until doubled, about 1½ hours. Knead again. Pinch off 2 pieces of dough, about the size of tennis balls and set aside. Shape remaining dough into a smooth flat cake about 23cm in diameter and

place on greased baking sheet. Roll small balls into long ropes. Cross ropes in the centre of the loaf. Place walnut halves over the top. Brush loaf with slightly beaten egg white. Cover, put in warm place until doubled in size. Bake at 160°C for 50 minutes or until it sounds hollow when thumped.

KOURABIEDES
(One of the favourite Christmas Greek biscuits)

250g butter
250g icing sugar
yolk of one egg
1½ tablespoons brandy or whisky
2½ cups sifted plain flour
½ cup very finely chopped almonds, lightly toasted
icing sugar for coating

Cream butter and sugar. Add egg and brandy/whisky. Add flour gradually. Add almonds. Chill dough for 20 minutes. Shape into crescents or balls. Bake at 160°C for 25-30 minutes. Toss in sugar when still warm.

A Greek Kalanda

85

Spain

It is a very festive time in Spain at Christmas. On Christmas Eve, as the stars come out, tiny oil lamps are lit in every house and, after Midnight Mass and Christmas dinner which follows, streets fill with dancers and onlookers. There is a special Christmas dance called the *Jota*, and the words and music have been handed down for hundreds of years. They dance to the sound of guitars and castanets.

Children in Spain think of the Three Wise Men as the gift bearers. Tradition has it that they arrive on January 6th, the date the Wise Men gave gifts to Jesus. Shoes are filled with straw or barley for the tired camels who must carry their riders through the busy night. By morning the camel food is gone and the presents have arrived.

It is the custom for three villagers to dress up as the Wise Men and pay a visit to the manger in the Village Square. The rest of the townspeople gather around to watch them pay homage to Jesus.

The Spanish especially honour the cow at Christmas because it is thought that when Mary gave birth to Jesus — that first Christmas — the cow in the stable breathed on the Baby Jesus to keep him warm.

TURON
(almond sweets — a special tradition in Spain at Christmas)

450g blanched toasted almonds
225g granulated sugar
125ml clear honey
1 packet marzipan

Combine almonds, sugar and honey in large saucepan. Set pan over very low heat. Cook until sugar dissolves and bring to boil. Cook three minutes, stirring constantly. Remove from heat and stir in marzipan. Beat thoroughly till smooth. Spoon into well-greased pan 15cm by 23cm. Mark into 4cm squares.

SOPA DE ALMONDRAS
(almond soup)

1⅓ cups blanched almonds
4 cloves garlic
4 tablespoons oil
salt to taste
4 tablespoons vinegar

Crush the almonds with the garlic, olive oil, and salt to a paste using a blender or mortar and pestle. Gradually add 10 cups water. Season and chill. Just before serving, stir in the vinegar. Serve garnished with grapes.

LECHONA ASADA VASCA
Roast Suckling Pig
(This is one of Spain's very festive dishes)

THE STUFFING
2 cups fresh white bread crumbs
2 tablespoons milk
4 medium onions, chopped finely
250g ground pork
250g ground veal
1 liver of suckling pig, chopped finely
2 tablespoons parsley chopped
1 teaspoon dried thyme and rosemary
½ cup dry sherry
¼ cup brandy
2 eggs
1 teaspoon salt
black pepper

6 eggs, hard-boiled and sliced
1 red eating apple

Wash the pig, pat it dry and rub it inside and out with salt.

To prepare the stuffing, put the bread crumbs in a large bowl and moisten them with the milk. Add the onions with the pork, veal and liver. Add the herbs, sherry, brandy, and eggs. Season, and mix everything thoroughly. Line the inside of the pig with the slices of egg, then pack it with the stuffing. Brush the pig with olive oil and roast for slightly under three hours. Serve the pig with a shiny red apple in its mouth. Whole roasted red and green peppers and dark-green watercress are often used as further garnish.

Come My Dear Old Lady

very rhythmical, all the way through

Come, my dear old lady, — With a lit-tle pres-ent — That you love so dear-ly, — of- fer it to Je-sus. We're weaving a garland of green lemon leaves for sweet Virgin Ma-ry, the Mother of God.

2. Kings of Orient riding,
   Cross the sandy desert,
   Bringing for the Baby
   Wine and cookies sweet.
   Refrain.

3. Kings of Orient riding,
   Guided by the starlight,
   Bringing to the Baby
   Gifts of love, this night.
   Refrain.

A Fire Is Started

The first three lines are very flowing and gentle.

Here in Bethle-hem this eve-ning, springs a mighty flame from hea-ven, Whom our sin-ful-ness will be con-sum-ing. And through whom we are for-giv-en.

Flash-ing and splash-ing, the fishes in the riv-er,
(water,)

Splash-ing and bow-ing to God from Heaven com-ing.
(prais-ing the Light from Heaven down-ing.)

2. In an old and humble stable,
   Blooms a spotless white Carnation,
   That becomes a lovely purple Lily,
   Sacrificed for our redemption.
      Refrain

3. Washing swaddling clothes for Jesus,
   Mary by a stream is singing.
   Birdlings chirp to her a joyful greeting,
   And the rippling brook is laughing.
      Refrain.

Denmark

According to legend, Christmas in Denmark is when a mischievous elf called Nisse can have his fun. He apparently lives in the lofts of old farmhouses and enjoys playing practical jokes. He wears grey woollen clothes, a red bonnet, red stockings and white clogs. Families leave him a bowl of rice pudding or porridge on Christmas Eve to keep his jokes within limits. But he is usually kind and helpful — helping on the farms and being especially good to children.

Christmas Eve dinner begins with rice pudding with a magic almond hidden inside. Whoever finds the almond receives a prize. Then they have goose, red cabbage and browned potatoes. After that lots of pastries and cakes.

The famous Danish tradition is the Christmas plate. In early days, rich Danes gave plates of biscuits and fruit as presents to their servants. These plates were often of the nicest and best kind and so were not for everyday use. So, collecting plates became a pleasant thing to do and nowadays special plates are made at Christmas for people to add to their collection.

Danish people take much trouble making their own decorations with bright paper, bits of wood and straw. The parents secretly decorate the tree, and children can only see it before dinner on Christmas Eve. The tree is then lit up and families gather around to sing carols and hymns.

Holland

St. Nicholas arrives early in Holland with his gifts, in November. He is dressed in Bishop's robes and journeys in a boat with his helper who is called Black Peter and who wears Spanish clothes. It is said that the pair live in Spain most of the year preparing lists of presents and writing down every child's behaviour in a very large book. Many people in Amsterdam go down to the docks to greet him. He mounts a snow-white horse and rides through the streets in a great parade, amid many festivities.

On December 5th — called Sinterklaas Eve — presents are given and received. The Dutch like to disguise their presents so as to make what emerges more exciting. A gift may, for example, be hidden inside a vegetable or in the middle of a cake. Sometimes, people have to follow strange clues before reaching their gift. Poems are read in Parliament too and the politicians give their speeches in rhymes for fun.

Christmas Day is a religious time, and the day is spent quietly with visits to Church. In the afternoon, people sit around the Christmas tree, sing carols and tell stories.

Farmers in Holland blow long horns at sunset each evening during the Christmas period, until the day after Christmas. These horns are blown over water wells which makes the sound extremely loud. This is done to announce the coming of Christmas.

St. Nicholas Alphabet Cookies.

ST. NICHOLAS ALPHABET COOKIES
(A Dutch Christmas tradition)

Use the biscuit recipe given for Christmas shape biscuits (page 101). Make a stencil of letters with cardboard. Cut biscuit dough around cardboard.

DUTCH ALMOND CHRISTMAS CAKE

1 250g packet frozen puff pastry
60g jam

Almond filling

120g butter
90g caster sugar
30g flour
2 eggs
120g ground almonds
30g crumbs
60g icing sugar

Thaw pastry and roll into an oblong 30cm long by 8cm wide and ¼cm thick. Cut into two strips the same size. Spread jam in middle of one strip, leaving 1cm for sealing.

Filling

Cream butter and sugar. Add eggs, almonds, crumbs and flour. Spread mixture over jam. Place other pastry strip on top. Seal edges. Let it stand for 20 minutes.

Slit top. Bake for 20 minutes at 200°C. Dust with icing sugar and reheat for 5 minutes. Cool. Cut into fingers.

Bright December Moon

Strongly Rhythmical

Bright De- cem-ber moon is beam-ing, Boys and girls now stop your play! For to- night's the wondrous eve- ning, Eve of good St Nich'las Day. O'er the roofs his horse un- shod, Brings us gifts or else the rod, O'er the roofs his horse un-shod, Brings us gifts or else the rod.

Good St. Nicholas

very bright

Good St Nich'las is in Hol-land once a- gain with his

horse and Pe-ter from sun-ny Spain. And

e — ven if he can't stay long,

We hope he'll stop to hear our song.

Dear St Nich-o-las the door is o-pen wide, For

you and Pe-ter to step in —— side. And we're

sing-ing, voices ringing, and our hearts re — joice, 'Cause the

Saint loves all good girls and good boys.

Poland

Most Polish people fast on Christmas Eve. When the first star appears in the sky, Polish families sit down to a large supper called *Wigilia* — no meat but many other things — beetroot soup, fish, cabbage, mushrooms and a sort of cake made from honey and poppy seeds. A vacant chair for the Holy Child always stands at the feast table. Another reason for the empty chair is for strangers, remembering the time Mary and Joseph called at the inn. The *oplatek*, a thin wafer of bread with the nativity scene stamped on it, is passed from person to person. Each person breaks a bit off before handing it to the next person. They then embrace and wish each other all the blessings of Christmas. After supper, the family all gather around the tree, and gifts are given.

Nativity puppet plays are popular in Poland, and are performed by local groups. St. Nicholas Day is on December 6th, and St. Nicholas, dressed in Bishop's clothes, gives out gifts.

On New Years Eve, the Polish people celebrate with a colourful carnival of some kind.

Russia

In Russia, the religious festival of Christmas is generally being replaced by the Festival of Winter, however the Christmas traditions are still kept up in some parts of the country.

In the traditional Russian Christmas which a few still keep up, special prayers are said and people fast, sometimes for 39 days, until January 6th — Christmas Eve — when the first evening star appears in the sky. Then begins a twelve-course supper in honour of each of the twelve Apostles — fish, beet soup (borsch), cabbage stuffed with millet, cooked dried fruit and much more.

Hay is spread on floors and tables to encourage horse feed to grow in the coming year and people make clucking noises to encourage their hens to lay eggs.

On Christmas Day, hymns are sung and people gather in the churches which are decorated with the usual Christmas trees, flowers and coloured lights. Christmas dinner includes a variety of different meats — goose and suckling pig are particular favourites.

Baboushka is a traditional Christmas figure who distributes presents to children. Her name means grandmother and the legend is that she declined to go with the Wise Men to see Jesus because of the cold weather (she was snug inside by the fire). However, she regretted not going and set off to try and catch up, filling her basket with presents. She never found Jesus, and that is why she visits each house, leaving toys for good children.

Yugoslavia

In Yugoslavia, children celebrate the second Sunday before Christmas as Mother's Day. The children creep in and tie her feet to her chair and shout, 'Mother's Day, Mother's Day, what will you pay to get away?' She then gives them presents. Children play the same trick on their father the week after.

The Yugoslavs who live in the country fear bad luck if their Christmas log burns out and so someone has to stand over the log all Christmas night to ensure it stays alight.

A Christmas cake, called *chestnitsa*, contains a gold or silver coin and apparently whoever gets it can expect lots of good luck.

The Yugoslavs eat roast pig as their Christmas fare and it must be carved a particular way, according to old customs.

Every household has a Christmas crib. Expeditions to the forests to gather moss with which to line the crib are another old custom. Quite often families would have an old-fashioned music box that plays Christmas carols.

Czechoslovakia

Christmas celebrations begin with the visit of St. Nicholas on December 6th, and end with the visit of the Three Kings.

In this country, a girl can tell her future, according to tradition, by putting a cherry twig in water on December 4th. If the twig blossoms before Christmas Eve, the girl will marry sometime during the year.

The famous King Wenceslas of the carol was a real King in Czechoslovakia. His goodness and Christian beliefs infuriated his mother, and his brother in jealousy murdered him on the Church steps. Before dying, he asked God's mercy for the brother's evil act. He became the patron saint of Czechoslovakia.

Christmas is a quiet and peaceful religious day here. They fast for one day, and have baked carp (a fish) for Christmas dinner.

St Nicholas visits, and brings good children gifts, and for children who are very bad, the devil is said to come with switches.

At midnight, most families go to Holy Mass or *Pasterka*, as it is called. On Christmas Day, the churches are filled with evergreens and Christmas trees. Celebrations go on for three days.

Rocking

2. Mary's little baby, sleep, sweetly sleep,
   Sleep in comfort, slumber deep;
   We will rock you, rock you, rock you;
   We will rock you, rock you, rock you:
   We will serve you all we can, Darling, darling little man.

Good King Wenceslas

2. 'Hither, page, and stand by me, if thou know'st it, telling,
   Yonder peasant, who is he? Where and what his dwelling?'
   'Sire, he lives a good league hence, underneath the mountain,
   Right against the forest fence, by Saint Agnes fountain.'

3. 'Bring me flesh, and bring me wine, bring me pine logs hither:
   Thou and I will see him dine, when we bear them thither.'
   Page and monarch, forth they went, forth they went together;
   Through the rude wind's wild lament and the bitter weather.

4. 'Sire, the night is darker now, and the wind blows stronger;
   Fails my heart, I know not how; I can go no longer.'
   'Mark my footsteps, good my page; tread thou in them boldly:
   Thou shalt find the winter's rage freeze thy blood less coldly.'

5. In his master's steps he trod, where the snow lay dinted;
   Heat was in the very sod which the saint had printed.
   Therefore, Christian men, be sure, wealth or rank possessing,
   Ye who now will be bless the poor, shall yourselves find blessing.

ACTIVITIES

Gift Ideas to Make

NOTEPADS

Cover squares (or circles) of card with sticky-backed plastic. Draw pictures on the outside or paste cut-outs on.

Trim writing paper to fit the squares (or even a little smaller).

Punch holes in the cardboard and paper and tie with ribbon.

SNOW SCENES IN A BOTTLE

Look for a nicely shaped jar with a lid. Paint the bottom of the jar a bright colour (you may have to go over it a few times).

Find some models to stick inside plastic Christmas tree or people, animals and houses. Or, find some unusual looking pebbles and shells, use blue plasticine for a river and make a nature scene. Glue firmly what you've found to the bottom of the jar. Fill with white vinegar and 2 teaspoons of coconut. Glue the top of the bottle on.

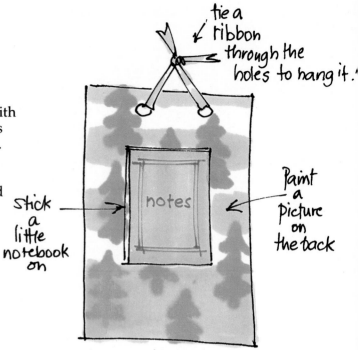

tie a ribbon through the holes to hang it.

Stick a little notebook on

Paint a picture on the back

if the lid has printing on it, paint it.

glue

Find some OLD FLOWER POTS (plastic or terracotta are both good). Paint patterns with bright paints or just one colour. Buy a little flower seedling (or if you're organised early enough, buy some seeds). Get some dirt. Plant the seedling/seeds.

Make a WINDOW BOX

You can buy cheap ones made out of foam material from a big store or perhaps a nursery. Paint it (if you want to).

Buy some seedlings or seeds. Plant.

To Dad!

read the instructions on the packet before you plant the seeds!

soil

screenings

hole

piece of broken pot covering hole

Other Ideas

DISGUISE PRESENTS (as they do in Holland)

Wrap up present in strange shapes or put present into a very big box when it is only a tiny thing.

OR

Just give a card with a clue to where it is so they have to search for it.

COLOURFUL CONTAINERS

Use empty margarine containers or plastic flower pots (wash them well first).
Cover with nice, coloured paper and fill with edibles such as chocolates or shortbread.
The taller containers can be used as pencil holders and you can cover some pencils with different coloured papers to go in them.

DECORATE A WASTEPAPER BASKET OR TRAY

Paint or glue pictures to the outside of the basket or to the surface of a tray.

See what you can make from things in the garden — make a collage on the top of a painted shoe box — for people to keep things in.

Start EARLY and KNIT
SOMETHING (even if it is summer).
Perhaps knit a scarf or a knee
warmer or anything else you can
think up.

Knitting!

POMANDERS

Get oranges, lemons, pears or apples
and lots of whole cloves. (You can
get these at any supermarket.)

Stick cloves into skin of fruit, line
by line, starting from the stalk. Try
not to leave any space between the
cloves. When they have dried out for
a day or two, tie ribbons around
them and give them away as
presents. People hang them in
clothes cupboards as they smell nice
and after a while so do the clothes!
(They will *not* go mouldy!)

pomanders

CHOCOLATE SURPRISES

A quick, delicious Christmas
confectionery to make that's as easy
as this.

Stone a bag of prunes (without
pulling the prune apart!).

Place as many almonds as there are
prunes on an oven tray and roast
until golden brown.

When the almonds have cooled
tuck one inside each prune.

Melt some dark chocolate over a
saucepan of very hot water (don't let
the water boil as the chocolate may
spoil).

Dip each prune into the melted
chocolate and let dry on a piece of
foil.

To give away, wrap each one in
coloured tin foil or cellophane and tie
with ribbons. Place in a pretty box or
jar.

CHRISTMAS SHORTBREADS

You will need:

150g plain flour
100g butter
50g sugar

Sift flour and sugar into mixing bowl.
Cut butter into small pieces and rub
into flour and sugar until the mixture
resembles breadcrumbs.

Form the dough into a ball and
press into a greased tin (flan tins
with removable bases are good to use
— ask Mum if she has one). Mark
out finger portions and prick the
surface with a fork.

Cook in the oven at 175°C for 45
minutes or until golden brown. Half-
way through the cooking time, turn
the oven down a bit.

Sprinkle with caster sugar and let
cool. To give away, put in nice jar
and decorate with bright ribbon.

shortbreads

CHRISTMAS PAPERWEIGHTS

You'll need some small rocks
felt scraps
poster paints
glue

Paint the rocks bright colours. Let dry.

Outline the Christmas design (or just a decorative design) on the felt. For example, draw a tree on green felt and the round ornaments on red, yellow, blue. Cut out the designs. Glue design on one side of the rock. Glue a piece of felt on the bottom so that it rests softly on the table.

BRIGHTEN UP YOUR RUBBISH BIN

Paint your galvanized iron rubbish bin a glossy bright colour. It will brighten up your street too!

DO SOME CARPENTRY

Make a tool box for Dad or Mum.

Find some wood and nails or get a wooden fruit box from the fruiterer. Make separate compartments for different tools. Paint it with 'Tool Box' painted on outside. Decorate any way you like.

WREATHS (to give away or to hang somewhere in your house)

Buy some large paper plates. Cut out the centre and throw away — you only need the rim.

Stick on some tinsel with staples or some sticky tape. Then attach (with staples or tape) brightly wrapped sweets.

potato cutting

GIFT WRAPPING

Make your own wrapping paper — buy white or plain coloured paper.

Mix paint with wall-paper paste to make mixture really thick.

Cut potato in half — carve design on the cut side. Dip in ink or paint.

Press potato print onto paper. You could use corks instead of potato and cut out a shape with a knife on one end — dip in ink.

Cut out stars, leaves, Christmas trees and other interesting shapes from cardboard and trace around them onto the blank paper. Then colour them in.

GIFT TAGS

Use a leaf (perhaps a gum leaf) and trace shape onto cardboard. Cut out shape and colour in, or do a decorative border.

GIFT BOXES

Paint old boxes gold or silver. Tie them up with ribbon and you don't have to wrap the present up with paper!

SILVER FOIL WRAP

Wrap up some gifts with silver foil — these look very dramatic and Christmassy.

PEPPERMINT CREAMS

1 egg white
325g sieved icing sugar
Peppermint essence (few drops)

Whisk egg white until frothy. Gradually add ⅔ of the icing sugar. When throughly mixed add a few drops of peppermint essence.

Turn the mixture out on to a board and mix in remaining icing sugar. Taste a little of it to see if it is pepperminty enough . . . if not add a few more drops of essence. Shape into oblongs 2cm thick. Cut into ½cm thick rounds. To make them even more delicious, dip each peppermint cream into melted cooking chocolate. Refrigerate.
To give away as gifts, wrap each one in coloured cellophane.

peppermint Creams

Make LITTLE CHRISTMAS PUDDINGS (an uncooked recipe)

These could be made as presents to give away, or just to eat at Christmas time.

1 cup powdered milk
1 cup coconut
1 cup mixed fruit
1 cup icing sugar
1½ cups rice bubbles
125g copha

Using a large bowl, mix together the milk and sugar. Sift the powdered milk and icing sugar into the bowl. Add the fruit, rice bubbles and coconut and stir. Melt the copha and add to what is in the bowl. Stir well. Press into little bowls or containers. Place in refrigerator to set. Wrap up in cellophane if to be given away.

CHRISTMAS CARDS

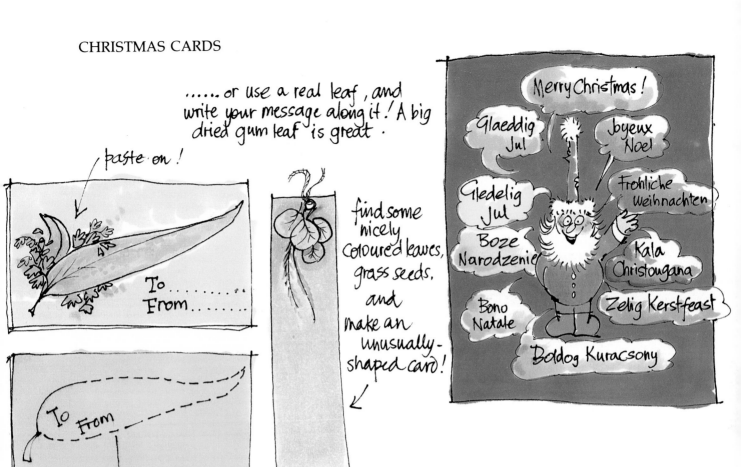

...... or use a real leaf, and write your message along it! A big dried gum leaf is great.

paste on!

To............
From........

To From

Cut out card

find some nicely coloured leaves, grass seeds, and make an unusually-shaped card!

Merry Christmas!

Glaeddig Jul

Joyeux Noel

Gledelig Jul

Frohliche Weihnachten

Boze Narodzenie

Kala Christougana

Bono Natale

Zelig Kerstfeest

Boldog Kuracsony

You can use all sorts of things to decorate plain cardboard or paper — ribbon, glitter, coloured wool, braid, pencils, pens, paints.

Press holly leaves or gum leaves for a few days in a heavy book until flat. Paint with clear nail varnish or gold or silver paint. Stick on with glue.

Use last year's cards if they've been kept and cut out bits of them that are nice and stick on to plain paper or cardboard.

Make cards yourself and write greetings in different languages on them, e.g., Happy Christmas in Italian — Buon Natale, Happy Christmas in Dutch — Vrolyk Kerstfeest.

Make your own cards with something Australian about them — perhaps funny ones, e.g., Father Christmas at the beach.

Cut stencils (star or tree or leaf shapes) and spatter paint with an old toothbrush onto cards, boxes, and paper.

Look up Christmas poems, choose some good lines and write them onto the cards.

Write your own poems and print them inside your cards.

Put inside your cards, messages especially for one particular person, e.g., to Mum with a promise to tidy room once a month; or to brother or sister to cook chocolate cake (or whatever their favourite cake might be).

More Decorations

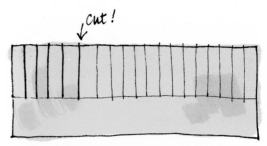

cut!

PAPER CHAINS

Use coloured paper in 2 or 3 different colours. Cut lots of strips about 2cm wide and 12-15cm long. Take one strip and glue one inside the other.

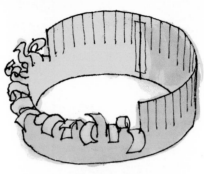

PAPER HATS

Find a piece of coloured paper that will go around the head. Rule your paper like an exercise book with lines about 1cm apart. Cut along the lines (but not to the end). Leave about 5cm for the band around your head. Roll into a circle. Staple or glue the ends together. Curl the cut strips so that they stand out on funny angles.

Make crowns (they are very Christmassy). Cut out a long piece of coloured paper to fit the head. Cut in zig-zag fashion along one side. Staple or glue ends.

Make dome-shaped decorative hats. Find different coloured papers. Cut one long strip to fit head. Join ends. Stick to rim piece other strips of paper bent in curves to fit the top of the head. Decorate with patterns or glitter.

you could paste some glitter here!

POPCORN CHAINS (American custom)

Buy popcorn (already cooked stuff). Get needle and thread. Double the cotton (to make it strong). Thread pieces of corn onto the string. You'll have a chain! Knot cotton at end of chain.

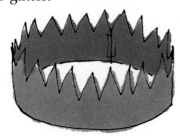

popcorn chain

Decorating Tree

star

reindeer

angel

Cotton wool

SHAPES OUT OF PIPE CLEANERS

You could make shapes of stars and bells. Perhaps wrap some tinsel around them to make them more colourful.

DECORATE BALLOONS

Use your textas or paint.
Draw stars and other Christmas things or perhaps do funny faces.

COVER PING-PONG BALLS
(or anything small and round you don't want) with silver foil

Stick a bit of ribbon, wire or string to the top to hang it with.

PAINT PINE-CONES silver, gold or some other colour.

MAKE STAR out of silver foil.

MAKE STREAMERS

Buy crepe paper — white and other colours that you like. Unfold it and cut along longest edge to make thin strips.

blow out the egg!

EGG SHELLS

Prick eggs with pin at both ends. Drain out egg by blowing hard through hole in egg. Rinse. Knot one end of elastic. Poke through hole. Paste on foil leaves where elastic comes out.
Decorate shells with glitter, paint, bits of material, lace or anything else that you can think of yourself.

PAINT GUM LEAVES AND GUM NUTS different colours — gold, silver or any other colour you like.

CHRISTMAS CONES

Paint icecream cones gold or sliver or whatever you like. Glue around the rim. Press Christmas tree ball onto cone — it will be like shiny icecream.
Decorate wet paint with glitter. Tie ribbon on and hang on tree.

POPCORN BALLS *(to eat)*

Cook some packet (uncooked) popcorn.
Mix ½ cup golden syrup, ½ teaspoon salt — cook in saucepan until golden syrup is runny.
Put butter on hands (to stop popcorn sticking). When mixture is cool enough to handle, shape into balls.
Wrap in foil.
Attach with green tape, ribbon or wire to hang them on the tree.

SPECIAL CHRISTMAS COOKY TREE

Find a nicely shaped branch of a tree. Paint it gold or silver. Put the branch in a pot, with some sand or dirt to help it stand up.

Hang cooky shapes (perhaps wrapped in foil to keep fresh) tied to the tree with tinsel. Perhaps wrap some of the cookies with foil and brightly coloured cellophane to make the tree look even more festive.

MAKE DOUGH FOR MODELLING

(Shape into decorations for Christmas tree or use to make presents such as pencil holders, bowl for flowers, paper weight or anything you can think of yourself.)

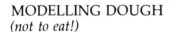

MODELLING DOUGH
(not to eat!)

1 cup cornflour
  (or plain flour)
1 cup salt
¾ cup water

Put into saucepan. Stir over low heat until ball is formed.

Let cool. Divide into lots. Add ink or other colourings. Make something! Let dry in cool place.

If you like, paint them with poster paint that has glue added to it.

MODELLING DOUGH *(to eat)*

185g butter
220g sugar
1 beaten egg
2½ cups flour
pinch salt

Cream butter and sugar. Add egg. Beat well. Mix in flour and salt. Divide up the dough into 3 portions. Add cocoa to one lot, and spices to the other, and leave the other portion plain. Roll out 1cm thick. Cook for 15 minutes at 190°C. Cut out Christmassy shapes and hang on tree.

SUGAR MICE OR PIGS

Buy fondant or make it. Here is how to make it:

Fondant Recipe

1½ cups caster sugar
½ tablespoon of melted butter
2 tablespoons cream or milk

Warm milk or cream and put in mixing bowl. Stir other ingredients in slowly and mix well. Add drop of cochineal to make fondant pink. Then knead together with your hands. Turn out onto board which has been dusted with icing sugar. Pat or roll out to about 5mm thick.

Mould shape of animal and tail with fondant. Use slivers of almond for ears. Use angelica for whiskers. Use little silver balls for eyes (or something else round like currants).

... or perhaps you can dress your biscuits up! (after they are cooked, of course!)

CHRISTMAS SHAPE BISCUITS

You will need:

1 cup plain flour
2 tablespoons butter
½ cup brown sugar
2 tablespoons golden syrup
1 teaspoon ginger

Mix all the ingredients together in a bowl. Form the dough into a ball and place in the refrigerator for ½ hour.

Roll out to a thickness of approx. ½cm.

Now the fun begins!
Cut out of cardboard — Christmas tree, bells, an angel, candles, Father Christmas . . . even Australian animals such as:— koalas, kangaroos and wombats. Anything that tickles your fancy!

Place the cut-outs on the dough and cut around them. Put on a greased oven tray and cook in the oven at 375°C for 15-20 minutes or until a light brown colour.

To make the biscuits more fun to eat, paint eyes, mouth, bells, etc., on with icing sugar mixed with a little boiling water and colouring.

CAKE WITH MAGIC ALMOND IN IT
(A Polish custom)

Cake Recipe
1½ cups flour
1 cup sugar
125g butter
2 eggs
½ cup milk
1 teaspoon vanilla (or, if *orange or lemon* cake preferred, add instead of vanilla, rind of one orange or lemon)
1 almond

Put flour and sugar into bowl. Mix together in another bowl the two eggs and the milk. Add this to flour and sugar. Mix well. Melt the butter and add. Lastly add the vanilla (or the rind), and do not forget the magic almond! Mix until smooth. Bake at 180°C for 40 minutes or until knife is clean when you poke it into the cake. Whoever gets the almond, gets good luck for a whole year!

In Mexico, a tiny doll is baked into a cake, and whoever gets it has to give a party. Perhaps you could try this custom. But do not use a plastic doll, it might melt!

113

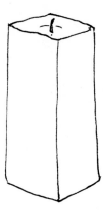

CHRISTMAS CANDLES

You will need:

Paraffin wax
wax crayons (green and red)
empty milk cartons
candle wick

Rinse out an empty milk carton and leave to dry.

In one of Mum's old saucepans melt, over a low heat, enough wax to fill approximately 2cm of the milk carton. Add to the melted wax a piece of red crayon and mix until the wax is bright, cherry Christmas red. Ask Mum or a brother or sister to hold the candle wick in the middle of the carton while you pour the wax in.
Leave to set.

Melt a small piece of wax (enough to make a thin stripe in the candle) and add a little of the green crayon to colour. Pour over the red wax and leave to set.

Next do a layer of red (approximately 1cm), and then another thin stripe of green. Make sure each layer is set before adding the next.

Fill the remainder of the carton with red wax and leave overnight. Carefully cut away the milk carton and set the candle with a little melted wax in a container (silver foil pie dishes work well). Trim with gold tinsel and leaves, holly and ribbons.

BONBONS

Find some old foil or plastic wrapping rolls and cut into about 12cm lengths. Place inside a brightly wrapped chocolate, perhaps fortunes, messages, jokes or any tiny little presents. Roll up with coloured crepe or tissue paper, leaving a good deal of paper over on either side of the tube from which to pull. Twist the paper around at each end of the tube, and tie pretty ribbon around ends. To make them look especially pretty and festive, buy some gold or silver paper and stick a thick strip around the tube part of the bonbon, leaving 2cm of the underneath paper showing. Decorate with glitter or anything you like.

HELP STIR THE PUDDING on the day Mum cooks it — you are entitled to a wish if you stir it three times!

MAKE A MANGER

Why not try and make an Australian-looking manger?

Find a good sized cardboard box. Use gum leaves and twigs for the stable floor and stick things from the garden over it. Make figures out of pipecleaners.

WRITE YOUR OWN CHRISTMAS PLAY

Perhaps put on a nativity play.
Try and write your own or use the story in this book.

Have a cast:
Mary
Joseph
Angel (can be innkeeper too)
3 Shepherds (who can double as the 3 Wise Men)

Have a crib:
Use sheets, blankets for costumes.
Make gold crowns for kings.

Perhaps use the King Wenceslas story — look up the words of the carol and get the story from that.

OR look in other collections of children's Christmas stories and base a little play on one you like.

Perhaps put on a play on Father Christmas coming to this country:
his observations about our Christmas;
him getting lost;
his reindeer needing drinks, feeling sick and hot — having to sack them and hire other animals.

CHRISTMAS BOOK

Start your own Christmas book at the beginning of December.
Shape it any way you like — square or round, fat or skinny.
Cover with Christmas paper.
Plan things to do. Make lists of gift ideas for your family and friends.
Perhaps put in stories, poems and pictures about Christmas that you like.
Copy poems from other books and make up some yourself.
Plan your Christmas holidays.

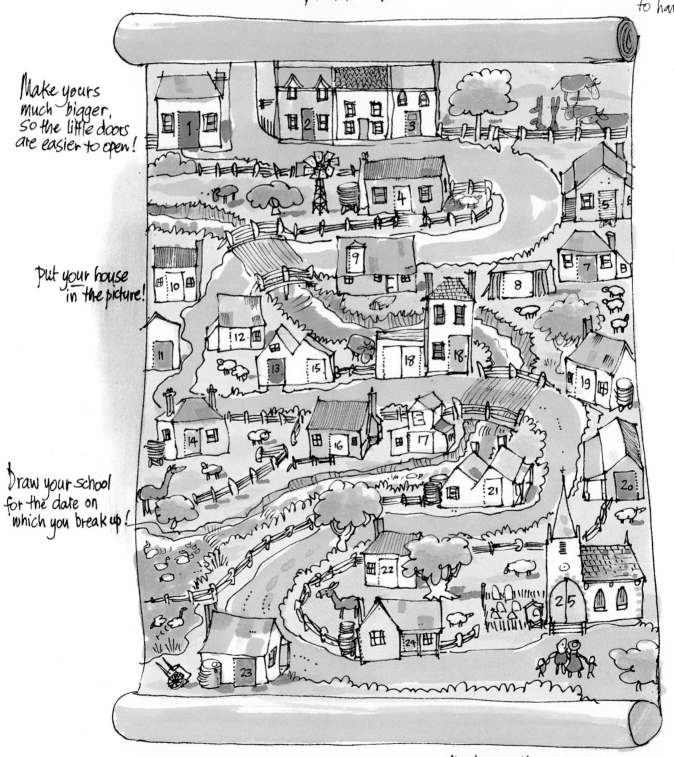

Pin it to a wooden rod to hang

Make yours much bigger, so the little doors are easier to open!

Put your house in the picture!

Draw your school for the date on which you break up!

Make 25th December a Church!

Advent Calendar

Making Advent calendars has long been a custom for children in many countries. Advent is the four Sundays before the birth of Christ — so roughly between the first of December and the 24th.

You could include in your calendar such dates as the school break-up, carols by candle-light, when to start your Christmas shopping, when to wrap your presents and any other dates important for the month.

Take two pieces of thick paper or cardboard, about the size of this book! Draw your village with the days from 1-25 on either doors or windows. Cut the little doors or windows so that they hinge on one side. Trace the cut-outs onto the second sheet, and draw a decoration in the spaces. Stick the sheets together and make sure the doors line up with the pictures!

Every morning, open a new door and see what is inside. A nice idea might be to make more than one Advent calendar and give one to an elderly person, or someone who is sick, or who you think just needs a surprise.

CAROL SINGING FROM HOUSE TO HOUSE
(This is a very popular custom in many countries throughout the world.)

RULES FOR CAROL SINGING

Don't let the dog out.
Don't trample on flower beds.
Ring door bell only once (though a pretty big ring).
Say "Happy Christmas" and "Thank you" when/if you are given something for singing.
Give good value — sing more than one song (but don't outstay your welcome!).
Perhaps make a lantern out of cardboard and put a torch inside (tie it so that it won't fall down). This might look good when standing on steps.

HAVE A FAMILY READING
Everyone must find a poem or story about Christmas to read. Have it on Christmas Eve.

Christmas Puppet Show

You will need:
Old socks
cardboard
buttons, scraps
of material, wool
coloured paper
scissors and glue
needle and thread

Christmas Eve is the perfect night to put on a puppet show for parents, friends and family telling the story of Christmas.

Mary and Joseph, and the Three Wise Men can be simply made using old socks. Sew buttons on for eyes, paint on the mouth, glue or stitch wool for hair and beards. Material can be used for clothes, coloured paper crowns for the Three Wise Men. Paint on their arms filled with presents for the baby Jesus.

Once all your puppets are made, work on the scenery for the stage. When Mary and Joseph set off to Bethlehem they travelled through desert — over hills scattered with trees and past shepherds with their sheep. Paint this scene on a piece of cardboard, cut it out and glue to a stick. When you tell the story, a friend could hold the scenery up while you show the puppets on their journey.

The same can be done with the stable, and with the shining star that leads the Wise Men. Another puppet could be made for Jesus, or paint the baby on cardboard as you have the stable and star, and glue to a stick.

Finish the puppet show with the beautiful carol 'Silent Night'.

IDEAS FOR THE THEATRE

Turn a table on its side.   The kitchen bench.
A fire screen draped with a towel or sheet.   The back of the couch.

STAINED GLASS WINDOWS

You will need:

A sheet of black cardboard
cellophane — all different colours
glue
scissors (a Stanley knife is better but
  check with Mum or Dad first)

Fold the cardboard in half (like a
Christmas card).

On the front draw Christmas
pictures with a pencil — angels,
stars, bells, a Christmas tree . . .
Father Christmas and his reindeer!
Keep the pictures simple so that they
are easy to cut out. Make sure you
leave space between each drawing
too! (1 centimetre at least).

With the cardboard still folded, cut
out the shapes (cut right through the
double thickness so that you can put
your fingers through the holes).

Now on the inside of the card glue
pieces of cellophane over the
pictures. Use a different colour on
each one. When this is done all you
need to do is glue the two sides of
the black cardboard together and
stick it up on your window!

Cut through

Stick coloured
cellophane
on the
back!

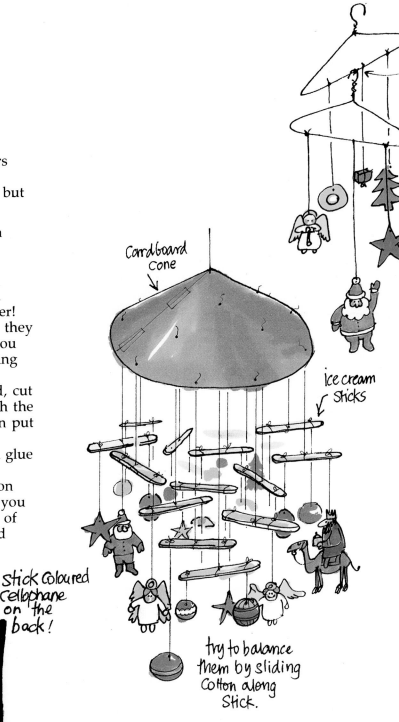

tie

Cardboard
Cone

ice cream
Sticks

try to balance
them by sliding
cotton along
Stick.

CHRISTMAS MOBILES

Perhaps use two coat hangers tied
together. Cover them with foil.

Find some shapes to suspend from
it — different glittery things. Perhaps
suspend edible shapes and sweets
from it with fine cotton.

Make a mobile out of icecream
sticks and dangle Christmassy things
from it.

Things to Do on Christmas Day

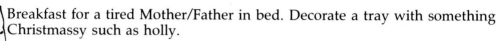

Breakfast for a tired Mother/Father in bed. Decorate a tray with something Christmassy such as holly.

Remember to take price tags off presents.

Sing carols through the door of parents' bedroom (but not too early!).

Sneak the wishbone from the turkey and make a wish.

Do remember to run in and say Happy Christmas to neighbours.

Leave something out for birds.

Give your dog, cat or bird something special for their dinner.

THINGS NOT TO DO ON CHRISTMAS DAY

Swim straight after dinner.

Put your fingers into parcels to find out the contents *before* opening time.

Wake parents too early.

Complain about presents.

Eat all your Christmas goodies in one go.

If you go to Church do not wriggle/giggle.

Give your mother a rolling pin (you never know what it may end up being used for.)

Give your Aunt Mabel a purple henna rinse for her hair (she may wonder why!).

Run away when Aunt wants to give you a big, sloppy kiss.

Drop the pudding!

Break your train/racing car/talking doll before breakfast.

Break window with new football.

Hit Gran on head with cricket ball.

Give lazy Father a paint roller.

Swallow the pudding coins (if there are any).

decorated breakfast!

Good Things to Do for Others at Christmas

Perhaps get some of your friends together and pay a visit to an old people's home or a hospital. Visit someone in your street who may be lonely at Christmas, perhaps someone with no family close by. Take little presents — perhaps some biscuits you have made. Sing some carols and have a talk.

Take along a little Christmas tree you could make out of, for example, a branch of a tree painted gold or silver with little things — decorations, and Christmas edibles hanging from it.

Why not prepare a White Christmas Parcel (this is an American custom). Organise a group of your friends to collect different little presents — food, toys — and take around to a family who might not have very much at Christmas.

Go through your old toys and choose some to take down to some place that gives presents out to children who would normally not receive very much at Christmas.

Try doing some good acts at home — being particularly nice to Mother — helping her in the kitchen, setting the table — there is a lot you could do!

LISTS

Presents you would like to give your teacher:
1.
2.
3.
4.

Your friends:
1.
2.
3.
4.

Your enemies!:
1.
2.
3.
4.

Presents I would like to give my teacher...

for my friends...

.... for my enemies...

Christmas Games

(Perhaps have a games evening with your friends on Christmas Eve)

TREASURE HUNT

Treasure hunt

The object is to find 'the treasure' (something Christmassy like a mince pie or a bonbon would be a good idea). The organizer makes up a series of clues and gives the players the first clue, something like 'Go to the place where much is said' (the telephone). Have the next clue placed there (but remember to have people replace the clues in the same place for the slower players). Think of lots of hard clues!

chinese whispers

CHINESE WHISPERS

Have a group seated in a circle.

Start off with a bit of information, a message, and whisper it to your neighbour.

See what the message comes out after it has gone all around the circle!

FORFEITS

(A traditional Christmas game especially in England)

Collect an item from each player. Each player must win back their possession by performing a forfeit, e.g. kissing everyone under the mistletoe!

CONSEQUENCES

Each player is given a long strip of paper and writes on the top an adjective or two describing a girl, e.g. 'bumbling, boring' then folds the top of the paper so as to cover the word. This is passed on to the person on his right who writes a girl's name and the word 'met'.

The pattern of writing one section, folding and passing the paper on to the next player continues. The players write again one or two adjectives describing a man, and the next player, the man's name, then where they met, what he said to her, what she said to him, what he gave her, and what happened to them — what the consequence was. Then each player reads out aloud what has been written on the strip of paper he has in his hands. Some very funny sentences and situations emerge!

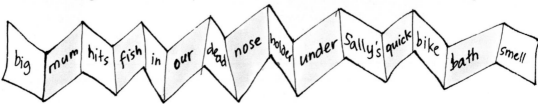

How 'Merry Christmas' is said around the World

CHINA	Kung Hsi Hsin Nien bing Chu Shen Tan
DENMARK	Glaedelig Jul
FRANCE	Joyeux Noël
GERMANY	Froehliche Weihnachten
GREECE	Kala Christougena
HOLLAND	Zalig Kerstfeast
HUNGARY	Boldog Kurascony
ITALY	Bono Natale
JAPAN	Meri Kurisumasu
NORWAY	Gledelig Jul
POLAND	Boze Narodzenie
SPAIN	Felicas Navidad
TURKEY	Noeliniz Ve Yeni Yiliniz Kutlu Olsun
WALES	Nadolig Llawen
IRELAND	Nodlaig mhaith chugnat

See if you can pronounce them!

INTERESTING SUPERSTITIONS

In Ireland, it is believed that gates of Heaven open at midnight on Christmas Eve. Those who die then can go straight to Heaven.

In Greece, some people burn their old shoes during the Christmas season to prevent misfortunes in the coming year.

If you eat a raw egg before eating anything else on Christmas morning, you will be able to carry heavy weights (of Christmas food!).

If you don't eat any plum pudding, you will lose a friend before next Christmas.

If you refuse mince pies at Christmas dinner (or during the day), you will have bad luck for a whole year — so eat up!

Eating an apple on the Eve of Christmas gives good health for a year.

In the Swedish countryside, from cock crow to daybreak on Christmas morning the trolls (wicked elves) roam about. So if in Sweden, stay indoors!

In Devonshire, England, a girl raps at the henhouse door on Christmas Eve. If a rooster crows, she will marry within the year.

You will have as many happy months in the coming year as the number of houses you eat mince pies in during Christmas.

Suggested Reading List

A Child's Christmas in Wales   Dylan Thomas, Dent
The Little Match Girl   Hans Christian Andersen
The Fir Tree   Hans Christian Andersen
A Christmas Carol   Charles Dickens
A Visit from St. Nicholas   the famous Christmas poem by Clement Clarke
    Moore. It starts off 'Twas the night before Christmas . . .'
The Little Shepherd Boy   Peggy Blakely, Black
Frosty the Snowman   Golden Books
Father Christmas   Raymond Briggs, Penguin
The Town that Forgot it was Christmas   Alf Proyson, Burke Books
A Christmas Card   Paul Theroux, Penguin, or hardback, Hamish Hamilton
King John's Christmas   in *Now We Are Six* by A. A. Milne
Bush Christmas   David Martin (poetry)
Happy Christmas   William Seymour and John Smith (a fascinating anthology
    suitable for older children)
The Sugar-Plum Christmas Book   J. Chapman, Hodder and Stoughton
    (anthology)
The Best Christmas Pageant Ever   B. Robinson, Faber and Faber (novel) also
    published as *The Worst Kids in the World* Hamlyn-Beaver Books
In the Week When Christmas Comes   E. Farjeon (poetry)
Christmas Daybreak   Christina Rossetti (poetry)

Acknowledgments

The publishers wish to acknowledge the invaluable assistance of Brigid Ryan for her meticulous research and compilation of the text; and of Richard Gerner for arranging and transcribing the music for the carols in this book.
The Three Drovers
Christmas Day
from AUSTRALIAN CHRISTMAS CAROLS
    Words by John Wheeler
    Music by William G. James
Chappell & Co. (Australia) Pty. Ltd.
Reproduced by permission of the copyright owner
Chappell & Co. (Australia) Pty. Ltd.